CW00739806

DAVID HAIG

David Haig has written
Theatre, London: *My Boy Jack* and *The Good Samaritan*, both
critically acclaimed. *My Boy Jack* was filmed for ITV, starring
David, Daniel Radcliffe and Kim Cattrall, and broadcast in
November 2007.

His distinguished acting career includes West End appearances
in *Yes, Prime Minister* (a transfer from Chichester); *Art*, *Dead
Funny* (a transfer from Hampstead), *Journey's End*, *The
Country Wife* and *The Sea*. At the National Theatre he appeared
in Alan Ayckbourn's *House/Garden*, and at the Royal Court in
Hitchcock Blonde and *The Recruiting Officer*. He has worked
extensively for the Royal Shakespeare Company, playing,
amongst others, Angelo in Trevor Nunn's production of
Measure for Measure. He won the Olivier Award for Best Actor
for *Our Country's Good* at the Royal Court, and received
nominations for *Mary Poppins* and *Donkeys' Years*, both in the
West End.

His television and film appearances include *Yes, Prime
Minister*, *Mo*, *The Wright Way*, *Four Weddings and a Funeral*,
The Thin Blue Line, *Talking Heads* and *Crime and Punishment*.

Other Titles from Nick Hern Books

David Haig

PRESSURE

NICK HERN BOOKS
London
www.nickhernbooks.co.uk

A Nick Hern Book

Pressure first published in Great Britain as a paperback original in 2014 by Nick Hern Books Limited, The Glasshouse, 49a Goldhawk Road, London W12 8QP

Pressure copyright © 2014 David Haig

David Haig has asserted his right to be identified as the author of this work

Cover photograph of David Haig as Dr James Stagg, by Drew Farrell

Designed and typeset by Nick Hern Books, London
Printed in Great Britain by Mimeo Ltd, Cambridgeshire PE29 6XX

A CIP catalogue record for this book is available from the British Library

ISBN 978 1 84842 388 6

Pressure was presented as a co-production between the Royal Lyceum Theatre Edinburgh and Chichester Festival Theatre, and first performed at The Lyceum on 1 May 2014. The cast was as follows:

DR JAMES STAGG	David Haig
YOUNG NAVAL RATING	Scott Gilmour
LIEUTENANT BATTERSBY/ CAPTAIN JOHNS	Anthony Bowers
COMMANDER FRANKLIN/ GENERAL 'TOOEY' SPAATZ	Gilly Gilchrist
ANDREW	Robert Jack
ELECTRICIAN/ADMIRAL BERTRAM 'BERTIE' RAMSAY	Michael Mackenzie
KAY SUMMERSBY	Laura Rogers
GENERAL DWIGHT D. 'IKE' EISENHOWER	Malcolm Sinclair
COLONEL IRVING P. KRICK	Tim Beckmann
AIR CHIEF MARSHALL SIR TRAFFORD LEIGH-MALLORY	Alister Cameron

Director	John Dove
Designer	Colin Richmond
Lighting Designer	Tim Mitchell
Deputy Lighting Designer	Guy Jones
Composer/Sound Designer	Philip Pinsky
Video Designer	Andrzej Goulding

The production transferred to the Minerva Theatre, Chichester, on 31 May 2014.

Characters

LIEUTENANT KAY SUMMERSBY
DR JAMES STAGG
ANDREW
NAVAL METEOROLOGIST
GENERAL DWIGHT D. 'IKE' EISENHOWER
COLONEL IRVING P. KRICK
CAPTAIN JOHNS
NAVAL RATING
ELECTRICIAN
SIR TRAFFORD LEIGH-MALLORY
ADMIRAL SIR BERTRAM 'BERTIE' RAMSAY
GENERAL 'TOOEY' SPAATZ
COMMANDER COLIN FRANKLIN
LIEUTENANT DAVID BATTERSBY

And a SECRETARY, *an* AIDE

This text went to press before the end of rehearsals and so may differ slightly from the play as performed.

ACT ONE

Scene One

1.00 p.m. Friday, 2 June 1944.

Southwick House, Portsmouth, England. Supreme Headquarters Allied Expeditionary Force.

A large room dominated by floor-to-ceiling French windows leading out to a small balcony. From the balcony, a view of the staggering Naval armada packed into Portsmouth Harbour – battleships, destroyers and landing craft, rail to rail, as far as the eye can see.

A stiflingly hot, summer afternoon. The sun streams through the windows, dust motes in the air. The room looks... transitional, as if waiting for someone to give it a purpose. Piles of wooden chairs, tables, a single telephone. There's a giant noticeboard, punctured by hundreds of drawing pins, but no notices. Leaning against this wall are two sets of library steps on wheels. There's an old upright piano in the corner.

LIEUTENANT KAY SUMMERSBY (*thirty-five years old*) *sits at a table by the window, sorting through a huge pile of correspondence. She is attractive, vivacious, the daughter of an Irish cavalry officer. She is also General Dwight D. 'Ike' Eisenhower's chauffeur, unofficial aide and confidante. She is dressed in the uniform of the Motor Transport Corps. The uniform is worn out. The seat of her skirt, shiny from constant driving, her jacket, faded.*

KAY, *like all the characters in the play, looks unslept. She lifts her head to feed off the warmth of the sun, but her peace is disturbed by the sudden roar of a fleet of bombers passing overhead, heading for the French coast. Their shadows blot out the sun.*

*The noise of the bombers masks the sound of the door opening.
An ordinary-looking man with a tidy moustache enters. He is
dusty, sweaty and is wearing an ill-fitting RAF uniform. He
carries a suitcase and a briefcase. This is* DR JAMES STAGG,
Chief Meteorological Officer for the Allied Forces.

He looks around him.

STAGG. I must be in the wrong room.

   KAY *jumps to her feet.*

KAY. Good afternoon, sir.

   STAGG *checks the number on the door.*

STAGG. Room six, first floor?

KAY. Yes, sir.

STAGG. Should you be in here?

KAY. I beg your pardon, sir.

STAGG. Should you be in here?

   He takes a sheet of paper out of his pocket and checks it.

   Room six. You'll need to clear your stuff out.

KAY (*demanding some sort of normal exchange*). How do you
   do. I'm Lieutenant Summersby.

STAGG. James Stagg. Is there only one telephone?

   I'll need more than that. Who should I talk to?

KAY. I'll find out.

STAGG (*looking around him. Shocked*). This is just a room.

KAY. I'll tell the General you've arrived.

STAGG. Which General?

KAY. General Eisenhower.

   A moment as STAGG *digests this.*

STAGG. He knows I'm arriving today.

KAY. Does he? It may have slipped his mind, he's a rather busy man.

STAGG. It won't have slipped his mind.

They stare at each other. STAGG, impassive. KAY, annoyed. She spins on her heel and leaves the room.

STAGG immediately removes KAY's correspondence from her table, dumping it on the floor, then he drags the table further into the room. He does the same with the other table and places a chair behind each.

He takes out a handkerchief and mops his brow, then opens the French windows and goes out onto the balcony. Shielding his eyes from the sun, he looks up at the sky, turning slowly on the spot, he looks north, east, south and west. As a cricketer would check the pitch, so the meteorologist checks the sky.

There is a knock on the door. STAGG returns from the balcony.

Come in.

A young man (ANDREW), excited and out of breath, enters in the uniform of a junior Air Force officer.

ANDREW. Welcome to Southwick House, Dr Stagg.

STAGG. Thank you.

STAGG claims one of the two tables as his own and starts unpacking his briefcase.

ANDREW. It's a great honour to meet you, sir.

STAGG says nothing. He sets out mathematical instruments and an array of pencils and coloured pens on his table.

I so enjoyed your paper on the Coriolis effect.

STAGG. It's a fascinating subject.

ANDREW. I'm a great admirer of the Bergen School. Upper-air structures.

STAGG. You're on the right lines then.

A young NAVAL METEOROLOGIST *hurries past the open door, but stops when he sees* ANDREW. *He hands* ANDREW *a piece of paper.*

NAVAL METEOROLOGIST. Latest thermograms, sir. Stevenson screen two.

ANDREW. Thank you.

The METEOROLOGIST *marches off.* (*Whenever the door is open, we're aware of voices, footsteps, doors slamming. A constant buzz of urgent activity.*)

(*To* STAGG.) I'm seconded to you, sir, for as long as you're here, if there's anything you need...

STAGG (*tension in his voice*). I need everything. Look at this room. I need an anemometer, a Stevenson screen, thermometers, barograph, barometer, telephones.

ANDREW. Admiral Ramsay has a forecast room downstairs, I'll see what I can find.

STAGG. I'd be grateful.

The NAVAL METEOROLOGIST *returns. He salutes sharply and hands* STAGG *a rolled-up chart.*

NAVAL METEOROLOGIST. Synoptic chart, sir. 1300 GMT.

STAGG *takes it.*

STAGG. Very good. How frequently are you producing charts?

NAVAL METEOROLOGIST. Every six hours, sir.

STAGG. Normal synoptic hours?

NAVAL METEOROLOGIST. Yes sir. 0100, 0700, 1300 and 1800.

STAGG. And intermediates at 0400, 1000 and 1600?

NAVAL METEOROLOGIST. Yes, sir.

STAGG. Thank you.

The METEOROLOGIST *leaves.* STAGG *wheels a set of
library steps to the giant notice board and climbs the steps.*

ANDREW. Shall I give you a hand, sir?

ANDREW *wheels the other steps over and climbs them.*
STAGG *hands him one end of the chart.*

I'm Andrew Carter, by the way. From the Met Office. Flight-
Lieutenant Carter I should say. They plonked me in the Air
Force, I've no idea why.

STAGG. No. (*A beat, then:*) I'm a Group Captain, I've never
been near an aeroplane.

STAGG *pins the top of the chart.*

ANDREW. Good journey, sir?

STAGG. Eighteen miles in seven and a half hours. An average
of 2.4 miles per hour.

ANDREW. The roads are impossibly busy.

Short silence.

Apparently, there are so many extra tanks and troops in the
country, only the barrage balloons stop Britain from sinking.

STAGG. Aye, so I heard. It's a fine, sunny day, I should have
walked.

ANDREW. Bit warm for walking, sir. We have a screen in the
grounds. The midday reading was 92.4.

STAGG *has finished pinning the chart.*

STAGG. You can let go.

*They release the chart which unrolls down the noticeboard.
It's a massive synoptic weather chart, stretching from
Newfoundland in the west to Central Europe in the east, from
Greenland in the north to the North African Coast in the
south. Written along the top is the caption: '1300 GMT
FRIDAY JUNE 2 1944.'*

For STAGG, *a new weather chart is like a Christmas present. He is instantly absorbed.* ANDREW *could be a million miles away.* STAGG *gently touches the chart, then traces his finger along one of the finely drawn lines.*

The chart could be as big as 12' x 4', big enough anyway to be seen clearly by the whole audience.

A high-ranking American officer appears in the open doorway below them. He takes a deep drag on an untipped Chesterfield and looks up at STAGG.

IKE. Good news?

STAGG *is too absorbed to reply. He glances briefly at the American officer, then turns back to the chart.* ANDREW, *on the other hand, scuttles down his library steps and slams to attention.*

ANDREW. Sir!

STAGG *continues to examine the chart, he places his hand over the Arctic Circle.*

STAGG (*half to himself*). Full of menace…

He climbs down a few steps and places his hand on the middle of the Atlantic Ocean.

…these are formidable…

He climbs off the steps and pushes them to one side. He places his hand over the Azores at the bottom of the chart.

…this is gentler… but interesting.

IKE. Good prognosis?

STAGG. When Colonel Krick arrives, we'll confer, then I believe I report to General Eisenhower.

IKE. I am General Eisenhower.

GENERAL DWIGHT D. 'IKE' EISENHOWER, *Allied Supreme Commander with sole responsibility for the D-Day landings.*

ANDREW *remains rigidly at attention.* STAGG *looks genuinely amazed.*

STAGG. I thought your voice was familiar. It's seeing you in the flesh, rather than just speaking to you on the telephone… and in your photographs you seem to have more hair than you actually have.

IKE *cannot find a suitable response.*

ANDREW (*to* STAGG). I'll see what I can find downstairs, Dr Stagg.

ANDREW *leaves.* IKE *closes the door. The buzz of voices in the corridor is muted.*

IKE *takes a packet of Chesterfields out of his pocket and lights a new one with the tip of the old.*

IKE. You got an ashtray in here?

STAGG. I've got very little of anything in here.

IKE. Not a problem. What do you need?

STAGG. Everything. A forecast room is a specific environment, this is just a room. It's certainly not good enough for the purpose.

IKE. Give Lieutenant Summersby a list of what you want.

IKE *walks towards the balcony.*

I need you to be close. I'm a couple of doors down.

Suddenly his right knee buckles under him.

Goddammit!!

He grabs one of the tables to support himself.

I have a knee. Goddamn!

IKE *gently flexes his leg.*

Boring! Cartilage. Football injury.

Gingerly, IKE *takes a couple of steps.*

Not talking about soccer, Dr Stagg, I'm talking about American football... more like your 'rugby', am I right? You ever play rugby?

STAGG. On occasion, sir.

IKE. If we ever get a spare moment, you're gonna tell me what in heck is going on in that game. I saw a match once and I sure as hell didn't know.

IKE *limps out onto the balcony. He stubs out the old Chesterfield with his foot.*

What a beautiful day. Flaming June!

What part of Scotland are you from?

STAGG. Dalkieth, sir. A wee town by Edinburgh.

IKE. God I love that city! First time I saw the castle on the rock – man! I'm from Kansas, I didn't see a hill till I was twelve years old.

IKE *takes a deep drag on the new cigarette and blows smoke into the blue sky. He looks down at Portsmouth Harbour.*

Seven thousand Naval vessels, Dr Stagg.

He turns back to STAGG.

Seven thousand vessels, one hundred and sixty thousand ground troops, two hundred thousand Naval personnel, fifteen hospital ships, eight thousand doctors, four airborne divisions. The biggest amphibious landing in history. And let me tell you, every piece of the jigsaw is in place. Every man and woman involved is ready and waiting. There's no more to learn. It's time to run with the ball. *But...* there is still one uncertainty, one imponderable that can stop this thing happening... that's why I've put you in this room. I want you right beside me for the next four days.

STAGG. I worry...

IKE. Not your job.

But STAGG *persists.*

STAGG. I worry that what you require of me is scientifically impossible.

IKE *waits for* STAGG *to continue.*

Long-term forecasting is only ever informed guesswork.

IKE. Monday isn't long term, for God's sake.

STAGG *checks his watch.*

STAGG. Sixty-five hours to go. In this part of the world, anything more than twenty-four hours is long term.

IKE. You listen to me, soldier. Your Met Office tells me you're a genius, you're tearing up the rulebooks. I don't care how you do it, but I'm relying on you and Colonel Krick to tell me if the weather's gonna be good on Monday.

STAGG. And on Sunday I will be able to offer you a degree of certainty.

IKE. Sunday's too late, goddammit. I need to know *now*. You got me?

STAGG *is silent.*

We've got one chance, Dr Stagg. One chance only to get this right.

IKE *walks towards the door, still limping slightly.*

Ask them to bring up a bed, you're gonna need it.

IKE *is almost out of the door, then he turns back.*

For the next four days, you're part of the family. Same team, same 'end zone'. Pardon me, wrong game. What would you call the end zone?

STAGG. The try line?

IKE. Sounds good. Same team, Stagg, same try line.

IKE *leaves, closing the door.* STAGG *mops his brow again. Another fleet of bombers roars overhead.*

STAGG *opens his suitcase and takes out a framed photograph of a heavily pregnant woman holding a child. He stares at the picture for a moment, then sits at his table, placing the photo in front of him.*

He concentrates on the chart on the wall and starts to make notes.

A knock on the door.

STAGG. Come.

KAY *enters.*

KAY. I've brought the 'little blue book'.

She flicks through to the correct page.

If we lost this, the Allies would probably lose the war! Your first meeting will be at 1500 hours. General Eisenhower, Air Chief Marshal Leigh-Mallory, Admiral Ramsay and General Spaatz will be present. They would like to meet you here. In this room.

STAGG *nods, concentrating on the chart. He changes pencil and draws a series of lines.*

Does that give you enough time?

STAGG. If Krick arrives soon.

Silence. STAGG *continues to draw lines, rub them out, refine them, make notes.* KAY *watches him work.* KAY *is not sure whether* STAGG *is talking to her, but suddenly he expresses his thoughts out loud.*

What he ignores is the third dimension, vertical structures, the upper air. This jet is thin, rapid, straight. No meandering, no Rossby waves. Freezing tongues of disruption pushing south. Vicious extrusions of cold air. He cannot ignore that.

KAY. Who's ignoring it?

STAGG *looks up, surprised. He had forgotten* KAY *was in the room. He stares at her, then returns to his work.*

STAGG. Sooner or later, the Arctic air will penetrate the westerly flow. L2 and L3 will be reinvigorated. But he won't see it.

STAGG falls silent again, making further notes. Then, suddenly:

I sent Flight Lieutenant Carter in search of equipment. There's been no foresight at all, the set-up's amateur! These tables should have sloping tops, I need paper, ink, pencils, thermometers, barograph, barometer… telephones, I must have more telephones.

KAY. I'll see what I can do.

STAGG. It's urgent.

KAY. Everything, Dr Stagg, is urgent. I'll do my best.

It's at this moment that KAY notices the correspondence she was working on, piled up on the floor. She marches over and starts to pick it up, placing it on top of a filing cabinet. She is furious, but her tone is controlled and polite.

Dr Stagg, this is the Supreme Allied Commander's personal correspondence. These are heartfelt, handwritten letters, sent from all over the world to General Eisenhower…

The NAVAL METEOROLOGIST enters and hands STAGG some papers.

NAVAL METEOROLOGIST. Radio soundings for the past twenty-four hours, sir. From weather ships *Dog*, *Baker* and *How*.

KAY continues brightly:

KAY.…As soon as I find another room in which I can work, I will do so.

STAGG (*to the* METEOROLOGIST). Thank you. I'd like all readings relating to L5 and the Azores anti-cyclone to be isolated and telephoned directly to me.

NAVAL METEOROLOGIST. Yes, sir.

KAY. In the meantime, for a few more hours, I would appreciate it if I could leave all this here. Somewhere safe... and not just...

The NAVAL METEOROLOGIST *leaves, closing the door.*

...dumped on the bloody floor.

STAGG *looks up, surprised by* KAY*'s sudden vehemence.*

STAGG. I'm sorry, what was your name?

KAY. Lieutenant Summersby, sir.

STAGG. Lieutenant Summersby, this is a forecast room.

A short icy silence.

KAY. Do you ever smile, Dr Stagg?

STAGG. Smile?

He considers the question deeply.

I hope I do. If there's something to smile about.

The door opens. A good-looking, but overfed man in his late thirties, breezes into the room. He has luxuriant hair and a well-trimmed moustache. This is COLONEL IRVING P. KRICK, *Chief Meteorologist for the United States Armed Forces and* STAGG*'s 'second-in-command'.*

(KRICK *was really the first 'celebrity' weatherman. Though a trained pianist, with a degree in physics, he was instinctively a salesman.*)

KRICK. God it's hot out there!

KRICK *wipes the sweat off his brow.*

Dr Stagg, I presume! Do we salute each other? I don't think so, do you?

They don't.

Fascinating to attach a face to the voice.

You're taller than I imagined.

STAGG. You're rounder than I imagined.

A momentary beat as KRICK *digests* STAGG*'s bluntness/rudeness.* KRICK *looks around him.*

KRICK. Jesus Christ, they call this a forecast room?

KAY *steps forward.*

KAY. Sir.

KRICK *smiles. He embraces* KAY *and kisses her on the cheek.*

KRICK. Hey! Kay Summersby! Long time, no see. Kay and I are old buddies. (*To* KAY.) Right, sweetheart? August '39, Stagg, David Selznik calls me in California, he's shooting a movie. Wants a forecast for a three-day period in Beverly Hills. The scene is the burning of Atlanta. Wants to burn the stage set to the ground. And of course he does *not want* precipitation. Great movie! Kay drove me and Ike to the London premiere. True, sweetheart?

KAY. Correct, sir.

At this point, the NAVAL METEOROLOGIST *and a* RATING *enter pushing trollies, laden high with large black leather folders – perhaps as many as a hundred. Each folder has a series of dates on it. E.G. 'MAY–JUNE 1912', 'MAY–JUNE 1923', etc.*

KRICK (*to the* METEOROLOGIST). Put 'em over there.

NAVAL METEOROLOGIST. Sir!

KRICK. Selznik said to me: 'Irv, I don't want to see a drop of rain for three days.' MGM give me dates, I forecast a dry spell, they shoot the scenes – beautiful weather, movie's a hit, I'm on the front page of the *LA Times* and I get to meet Clark Gable. Movie called *Gone with the Wind*. You see it, Stagg?

STAGG. No.

The METEOROLOGIST *and* RATING *leave.*

KAY. Did you meet Vivien Leigh?

KRICK. I did.

KAY. What was she like?

KRICK. Cute, of course. Kinda… remote… beautiful skin, but too fragile for my taste, she looked breakable.

KAY. How exciting!

STAGG *picks up one of* KRICK*'s folders.*

KRICK (*explaining the folders*). Analogues.

STAGG. I realise that.

KRICK. I guess you know, Kay, Stagg and I have been talking on the telephone since the middle of March. This is the first time we've actually met.

STAGG. Shall we start? The meeting is at 1500 hours.

The phone rings. STAGG *answers it.*

(*On phone.*) Stagg… one moment please…

STAGG *grabs paper and pencil.*

KRICK (*to* KAY). You still driving Ike round in a Buick?

KAY. No, the Buick died, the gears went haywire.

STAGG (*on phone*). 40.2 north…

KAY *focuses on* STAGG *as she and* KRICK *talk.*

KRICK. What do you drive now?

KAY. A Packard Clipper.

STAGG (*on phone*). 46.7 west…

KRICK. Good motor car?

KAY. The brakes are a perfect bore, I spend my life attaching bleeder hoses to the wheel cylinders.

STAGG (*on phone*). 1011 millibars… rising… 2 knots. Thank you.

STAGG *puts the phone down.*

L5 is moving north.

STAGG *goes to the chart and, with a red crayon, adjusts the position of storm L5 a fraction further north.*

A British Army Adjutant in his forties, CAPTAIN JOHNS, *appears at the door.*

CAPTAIN JOHNS. Lieutenant Summersby?

KAY. Would you excuse me, Colonel?

KRICK. Irving, please.

KAY *gets a card out of her pocket. She gives it to* STAGG.

KAY (*to* STAGG). Please ring this internal extension if you need to speak to General Eisenhower. He'd like you to call at any time, day or night, if it's important.

STAGG. Is this a direct line to General Eisenhower?

KAY. No, sir, it's a direct line to me.

They hold each other's gaze for a moment. STAGG *pockets the card.* KAY *marches smartly out of the room, followed by* CAPTAIN JOHNS.

KRICK. Now we can actually see each other, maybe things'll improve.

STAGG (*checking his watch*). Sixty-four hours. We should start.

STAGG *stands in front of the chart and begins his analysis.*

A family of four low-pressure centres, four aggressive storms, stretching from Jutland, L1 –

He points to L1 on the chart.

– across the Atlantic Ocean to L4 south of Nova Scotia. A fifth storm, L5, lurks here.

He points to L5.

KRICK. Already on the move.

STAGG. Aye, but yet to be drawn into the bosom of the family. We also have a formidable, unforgiving mass of high pressure extending a third of the way round the Arctic Circle, from the Rocky Mountains to the White Sea.

KRICK. Sure.

STAGG. Finally, an area of high pressure over the Azores...

He points to the anti-cyclone over the Azores.

KRICK. That's what interests me.

STAGG. ...gentler than its polar cousin, it's moving lethargically...

KRICK. Your word, not mine.

STAGG. ...north-eastward towards Europe. What you see on this chart is precisely what I anticipated...

KRICK. I'm not interested in what you anticipated.

STAGG. I mention that I was correct, as a statement of fact...

KRICK. But you had to tell me.

STAGG. ...To support the forecast I'm about to give.

KRICK. Just talk about the goddamn weather...

STAGG. You diminish yourself, Colonel Krick...

KRICK. Talk about the weather not yourself, okay?

STAGG. ...By accusing me of self-interest.

KRICK. Talk about the fucking weather, will ya?

Tense silence.

STAGG (*voice trembling with intensity*). If we continue like this, we will fail. We – will – FAIL. And thousands of men will die because of our failure.

KRICK. What is your forecast for D-Day?

STAGG *collects himself and begins his forecast.*

STAGG. My forecast is not only based on weather at the surface...

There's a knock on the door. STAGG *tries to ignore it.*

...I've also considered upper-air currents within the troposphere, at the tropopause, and in the lower stratosphere...

Another knock on the door.

One moment! The most powerful of these currents, measured two hours ago at twenty-eight thousand feet, is three hundred miles wide and three miles deep. I'll refer to it as the jet stream...

KRICK. There's no proof the jet stream exists.

STAGG. It definitely exists.

KRICK. Who says?

STAGG (*on his way to answer the door*). Last week two B17s flying from New York to Prestwick found the jet stream and cut their travel time by one third. The tail wind was measured at 120 knots.

KRICK. You're taking the word of two pilots? That's not proof, goddammit!

STAGG *opens the door, the* NAVAL METEOROLOGIST *hands him some papers.*

NAVAL METEOROLOGIST. More signals from *How* and *Dog*, sir.

The METEOROLOGIST *leaves.*

STAGG. Colonel Krick, you think two dimensionally. (*Glancing at the papers.*) L5 is still moving.

He puts the papers on his table.

You know as well as I do that upper-air structures determine weather at surface level.

KRICK. To an extent.

STAGG. And the jet stream is no exception. It is now moving very straight and very fast...

KRICK. Sure, but at twenty-eight thousand feet.

STAGG. ...driving storms 2, 3 and 4 at great speed towards Europe.

KRICK. Not from twenty-eight thousand feet it isn't.

STAGG. Because of the energy of this current, our storms are moving more rapidly than the surface chart would imply. L2 will move east or south-eastward. L3 will follow quickly, east-north-east to the latitude of Lerwick.

KRICK. Where the fuck's Lerwick?

STAGG (*pointing it out on the chart*). The capital of the Shetlands.

KRICK. Which is a thousand miles north of the English Channel.

STAGG. The speed of movement of these depressions...

KRICK. A thousand miles, Stagg!

STAGG.... will bring to southern England and the English Channel, a stream of humid air with considerable amounts of low cloud, substantial rainfall and, at times, strong winds.

KRICK. I don't think so.

STAGG. This weather is likely to last at least two to three days. Saturday, Sunday, and most likely Monday... D-Day.

KRICK. I don't agree.

STAGG. The poor weather on D-Day, will, I suggest, make the landings extremely problematic, if not impossible. Low cloud, base five hundred feet, seven to nine-tenths complete cover. Poor visibility. Considerable swell. Waves six to ten feet. Wind speeds, force five to six, occasionally, force seven.

STAGG *has finished*.

KRICK. You done?

KRICK *takes a chart from his black-leather folder and hands it to* STAGG.

Okay. This is the weather chart for June 2nd, 1923. And I could have given you June 3rd 1919, or June 10th 1926, all three identical to the chart on this wall.

STAGG. Not identical.

KRICK. Virtually.

He points to the main chart on the wall.

Same depressions in the Atlantic. Same ridge of high
pressure over the Arctic Circle. And *most* importantly, the
same high pressure over the Azores... here.

He taps the Azores on the chart, then hands STAGG *another
analogue chart.*

...now move forward three days... to June *5th* 1923, D-Day
if you like, but twenty-one years ago.

He uses the main chart to demonstrate.

The ridge of high pressure over the Azores has strengthened
and pushed north-eastwards, pressing L2, 3 and 4 northwards
towards Iceland, thereby *protecting* the English Channel
from any direct onslaught by the Atlantic storms.

STAGG. Because the storms in 1923 were less intense.

KRICK. Not true. It's a classic battle between good and evil!
And let me tell you, Stagg, 'good' will prevail, as it did in
1919, '23 and '26. The proof is in the past. I anticipate calm
seas and clear skies on Monday – perfect conditions for the
Normandy landings.

Complete impasse. The two men stare at each other.

STAGG. In less than half an hour, I have to present an agreed
forecast to General Eisenhower. How can I do that when you
predict a glorious sunny day, and I predict storm-force winds
and rain. For the sake of the three hundred and fifty thousand
men who will cross the Channel on Monday, is there no
room for compromise?

KRICK. You tell me.

STAGG. Nothing would please me more than to agree with you,
but I can't. Your system is flawed...

KRICK. Bullshit!

STAGG. You have to think three-dimensionally. Surface
weather is not enough on its own.

KRICK. Let me tell you something, thousands of lives were saved in the Torch campaign, using analogues.

STAGG. You were lucky.

KRICK (*incensed*). I was not goddamned lucky! The Air Force and the Army needed long-term predictions – and they got them, and the predictions were right – every time.

STAGG. Except, of course, at Anzio. On that occasion your analogues were completely inaccurate, if they had followed your advice not mine, the landings would never have happened.

KRICK *and* STAGG *are boiling with frustration.*

We need to compromise.

KRICK. Compromise requires movement on both sides.

STAGG *gestures to* KRICK*'s leather folders full of weather charts going back fifty years.*

STAGG. Where are those charts from?

KRICK. What do you mean, 'where are they from'?

STAGG. They come from Washington DC. Drawn up by men and women who've never even been to Europe, let alone stood on a beach on the south coast of England. Have you ever done that, Colonel Krick? Have you ever been to the beaches of Hastings, or Brighton, or Portsmouth?

KRICK. I'm a physicist, Stagg, not a tourist.

STAGG. Ten o'clock in the morning it's baking hot, the beach is packed. By midday, there's a howling wind and the Punch and Judy man has packed up for the day.

KRICK. Jesus Christ!

STAGG. By two o'clock, the rain is horizontal, but by four o'clock... the sun is beating down again and it's eighty degrees. Nothing is predictable about British weather, that's why we love to talk about it.

KRICK. So, I have to get wet to know why it's raining?

STAGG. We're not on a film set in Beverly Hills, we are in northern Europe. Your analogue charts do not even begin to replicate what we have here.

KRICK. In identical scenarios in the past...

STAGG. Not identical...

KRICK. ...high pressure over the Azores repelled similar storms...

STAGG. Lesser storms.

KRICK. ...and drove them north. Scotland may have terrible weather on D-Day, the Channel will be fine and sunny.

Impasse again.

STAGG. Colonel Krick, it's Friday. The invasion is on Monday. What we decide now, *together*, will determine whether the invasion goes ahead or not. Let's remember why we've been picked. You're American. I'm British. If D-Day fails because of a bad weather forecast, it fails because of an *Allied* blunder, no *one* side must be seen to be blamed. Hence the need for us to agree – (*Urgent.*) on – some – level.

Long silence. KRICK *doesn't budge an inch.* STAGG *checks his watch.*

(*Suddenly on his feet, active.*) I've decided to meet the Commanders-in-Chief alone.

KRICK. You can't do that.

STAGG. The last thing Eisenhower needs at the moment is uncertainty.

KRICK. Or a mistake.

STAGG. Final decision.

KRICK. He needs to know there's more than one possible outcome.

STAGG. The forecast for D-Day is my responsibility.

KRICK. I'm gonna talk to Spaatz.

STAGG. By all means.

KRICK. Have you any idea of the consequences of postponement?

STAGG. Of course I have.

KRICK. Can you imagine the effect on morale?

STAGG. I am offering the C-in-Cs a weather forecast in good faith. It's up to them how they choose to respond to it.

KRICK (*deliberately*). Which is why they should be made aware of both arguments.

A final impasse.

STAGG. We'll reconvene at midnight for the next chart.

A beat in which KRICK *decides whether to object further. He doesn't. He goes to the door and opens it, he's confronted by* ANDREW *coming the other way, laden with meteorological equipment.* KRICK *barges past him.* ANDREW *staggers into the room, dumping the equipment on the floor.*

STAGG *appears oblivious to* ANDREW*'s presence, absorbed in his own thoughts.*

ANDREW. We've done rather well, sir… Where shall I put these?

STAGG (*suddenly active, urgent*). Come and look at this chart with me.

STAGG *practically drags* ANDREW *to the chart.*

I want your opinion.

ANDREW. I don't think I'm…

STAGG. I want to know what you think. Will this anti-cyclone over the Azores extend and deflect 2, 3 and 4?

ANDREW. I don't really think I'm the one to…

STAGG. I want to know what you think.

ANDREW *leans nervously into the chart.*

ANDREW. I think it… I think it could go either way.

STAGG. It could, so what would tilt the balance one way or the other?

   ANDREW *looks reluctant to be drawn in, but carries on.*

ANDREW. I would look at the intensity of the Atlantic storms…

STAGG. Aye, and…?

   The NAVAL METEOROLOGIST *and the* NAVAL RATING *enter, carrying more equipment.*

NAVAL METEOROLOGIST (*to* STAGG). Where do you want these, sir?

STAGG. On the floor. Anywhere. (*To* ANDREW.) And…?

ANDREW. I would look at the strength of the pressure gradient…

STAGG. Aye.

ANDREW.…and the thickness charts…

STAGG. Good. (*To the* METEOROLOGIST.) That'll be all. (*To* ANDREW.) What else?

ANDREW.…the velocity of the upper winds.

STAGG. Exactly!

   STAGG *picks up the papers that were delivered earlier in the scene. He reads out a series of figures.*

   Look at these. 22,000 feet – 115 knots. 26,000 feet – 120 knots. 28,000 feet – 135 knots. Extraordinary readings. Readings you'd associate with December not June.

ANDREW. They could have a huge impact on the speed of the storms.

STAGG. But how do I convince someone who doesn't even believe the jet stream exists? How do I persuade General Eisenhower that the man he trusts relies on a fallacious, archaic system?

ANDREW. I'm sure you'll find a way, sir.

STAGG. Are you? I'm not. And should I be trying to persuade him anyway? There's only one other date this year when spring tide coincides with first light, and on that night there's no full moon. Can he afford to postpone? He may *have* to go on Monday.

ANDREW. They should listen to you, of all people.

STAGG. Why? Would you, in their shoes? Not a cloud in the sky, not a breath of wind. The last thing they want to hear is what I've got to tell them... (*A sudden change of tone, honest.*) And I may be wrong, his anti-cyclone is a plausible theory, he's always been lucky. I'm a scientist, for God's sake, not a gambler. But that's what they're making us do... gamble, with three hundred and fifty thousand lives at stake.

ANDREW (*disappointed in his hero*). It's more than gambling, sir.

STAGG picks a barometer off the top of the pile of equipment and hangs it from an exposed nail on the wall. STAGG taps the glass and adjusts the brass arrow.

STAGG. Set up the barograph, will you?

ANDREW. Sir.

A sixty-year-old civilian ELECTRICIAN appears in the doorway, carrying two telephones and a mass of cable.

ELECTRICIAN. Two telephones.

STAGG. How long will it take?

ELECTRICIAN. Five minutes.

STAGG. If you're quick.

A sudden thought strikes STAGG. He takes KAY's card out of his pocket and rings her internal extension.

STAGG (*on phone*). Lieutenant Summersby... I need a typewriter urgently... for God's sake, do you really care if I say please or thank you every time I ask you for something? This isn't an English tea party!

KAY *obviously stands her ground, because:*

...Please!

He slams down the telephone.

ELECTRICIAN. Where d'you want them?

STAGG *taps* KRICK*'s table.*

STAGG. On this table.

STAGG *sits at his table and starts writing his forecast for Eisenhower.*

The ELECTRICIAN *places the phones on* KRICK*'s table. He extends cable from the phones to a point on the wall.*

CAPTAIN JOHNS *pops his head round the door.*

CAPTAIN JOHNS. The C-in-Cs have arrived. They'd like to start in ten minutes.

CAPTAIN JOHNS *goes.*

ELECTRICIAN. Can't come a moment too soon for me, mate.

STAGG. I'm sorry, what can't?

ELECTRICIAN. The invasion. The sooner the better.

The NAVAL METEOROLOGIST *returns with more equipment: paper, pens, pencils, ink, etc.*

NAVAL METEOROLOGIST (*to* STAGG). And these, sir?

STAGG. On the table please.

While the ELECTRICIAN *talks,* ANDREW *sets up the barograph,* STAGG *writes and the* METEOROLOGIST *drops off the equipment and leaves again.*

ELECTRICIAN. They phoned me a week ago, I live in Portsmouth, they said could I come up to Southwick House and put in some extra telephone lines.

STAGG (*not interested, he concentrates on writing his forecast*). Really?

ELECTRICIAN. I said yeah if you want, I've given it all up really, but I'll do it if you pay me. They told me the hourly rate, I thought blimey I've never been paid that before, so I said yes. I couldn't work out why they picked me. I know now of course. Anyway I come up here and I put the extra lines in, in an office just down the corridor from here as it happens, and on the wall there's a huge, coloured map of Normandy, you know with tiny wooden boats crossing the Channel to these beaches, and all the beaches are labelled: Juno, Sword, is it? I can't remember the other names, but... anyway I thought: aaah, so that's where it's going to be. It's Normandy, not Calais at all. So I finish putting in the lines, pack up my stuff, go to the door, open it and there's two 'Snowballs' waiting for me, and they say: sorry, you can't go home, apologies for the inconvenience but you know too much, you're officially detained here till after the invasion. I said when's that? They said: none of your business.

STAGG (*not listening*). Really?

ELECTRICIAN. I bumped into the lads who put up the map of Normandy actually, they're here! Chad Valley the toy manufacturers made the map and sent these two chippies in to put it up and they were detained too! They've been here longer than me. I wish they'd hurry up and invade, I wanna go home. I know why they picked me of course, I'm sixty, retired, no wife, no kids, no one'd know I'm missing. They had it all worked out. There you are, mate, all done.

He lifts the receivers on both phones and listens for the dialling tone.

All working. Internal calls only, of course, till after the invasion. What's your job?

STAGG *says nothing.*

All right, fair enough.

At this moment, KAY *walks in, carrying a typewriter.*

Let me know if there's any problems.

The ELECTRICIAN *picks up his tools.*

(*To* KAY.) All right, love?

KAY. Yes thanks.

The ELECTRICIAN *leaves.*

One typewriter.

STAGG. He didn't stop talking from the moment he walked in to the moment he left.

KAY. What about?

STAGG. I've no idea. I wasn't listening.

STAGG *takes the typewriter from* KAY. *He puts it on a table. He mumbles under his breath:*

Thank you.

KAY. Not at all.

STAGG *examines the typewriter. He needs paper and carbon paper. He finds paper in his briefcase.* ANDREW *brings him carbon. The phone rings.* STAGG *answers it.*

STAGG (*on phone*). Stagg. One moment...

STAGG *hands the phone to* ANDREW.

Take this down, will you.

ANDREW *grabs paper and pencil.*

ANDREW (*on phone*). Hello... 41.2 north. Yes. 46.1 west. 1010. Thank you. Falling. 2 knots. 71 degrees.

STAGG *tries to sandwich carbons between paper and insert them into the typewriter.*

ANDREW *puts down the phone.*

STAGG. L5?

ANDREW. Yes, sir.

STAGG. Mark it up, will you.

ANDREW. Me?

STAGG. Aye.

ANDREW goes to the chart and adjusts the position of L5. The storm is creeping northward.

STAGG is battling with the typewriter. The first pieces of paper are a disaster, crumpled up before he's even started.

He rips them out, scrumples them and throws them on the floor. The second attempt is just as bad, he rips them out and throws them away. He's becoming increasingly frustrated.

KAY. Would you like some help?

STAGG presses a key and the carriage shoots across to the left. He pushes it back to the right and types a couple of words.

STAGG. This machine's out of the Ark! I should have been allocated a typist as soon as I arrived.

KAY. Will I do?

STAGG. Do you understand these machines?

KAY. More or less. I'm getting better.

The carriage shoots across again. STAGG *despairs.*

STAGG. It has a life of its own.

CAPTAIN JOHNS *knocks and enters.*

CAPTAIN JOHNS. They're ready for you, sir.

STAGG stands up, pushing the typewriter away and scraping his chair back. CAPTAIN JOHNS *leaves.* STAGG *walks to the French windows and stares out at the late-afternoon sun, at the serene sky.*

He turns back to KAY.

STAGG. The weather gods are toying with us.

A beat, then:

KAY. Four copies?

STAGG. Is that possible?

KAY. We can try.

KAY sits at the table and pulls the typewriter towards her. Efficiently, quickly, she sandwiches three carbons between four sheets of paper. She inserts them into the typewriter.

STAGG walks to the table and pushes a piece of paper, the handwritten forecast, towards her. She puts on a pair of reading glasses and starts to type.

STAGG is astonished by her typing speed. Her fingers fly over the keys. For a moment he and ANDREW watch her in silence. Then:

ANDREW. Anything else I can do, sir?

STAGG. Will you see that all upper-air data, in or out of synoptic hours, is sent directly to me. I want to be notified of any changes in upper-wind velocity.

ANDREW. Yes, sir.

STAGG. What is your extension?

ANDREW. 231.

STAGG. I'll telephone you if I need you...

ANDREW. Good luck, sir.

ANDREW slips out of the room. KAY is typing away. STAGG notices her hands are black.

Your hands.

She holds them up in front of her face and wiggles her fingers for a second.

KAY. Oil. Impossible to get it off.

She returns to her typing. STAGG checks his watch. Silence, save the clack of the typewriter.

STAGG goes to the chart and examines it. He talks (half to himself, half to the absent KRICK) as KAY types.

STAGG. 1010, 1013, 1014, it's not enough! (*Questioning himself for a second.*) Is it? Surely not. If the jet was further north you might have a point. No, not even then! Use your eyes, man, use your bloody eyes! Look at L2, for God's sake.

KAY finishes typing. She removes her specs, pulls the paper out of the typewriter and extracts the carbons. She examines the fourth carbon copy.

KAY. The fourth is rather faint. Give it to Leigh-Mallory, make him work for his supper.

KAY hands the four copies to STAGG.

They won't like the forecast.

STAGG. Nor do I.

KAY checks her watch, then goes to the door.

KAY. I'll tell them you're ready. Don't take anything Leigh-Mallory says personally, he's got even worse manners than you.

She leaves, closing the door. STAGG sets out some chairs, then stands in front of the chart, clutching his notes. He waits… and waits.

Eventually the door opens. IKE leads the way, followed by GENERAL 'TOOEY' SPAATZ, ADMIRAL SIR BERTRAM 'BERTIE' RAMSAY and AIR CHIEF MARSHAL SIR TRAFFORD LEIGH-MALLORY. CAPTAIN JOHNS, another AIDE and a SECRETARY, bring up the rear.

STAGG is extremely nervous.

IKE (*introducing everyone*). Group Captain Stagg – this is Admiral Ramsay, Commander-in-Chief, Allied Naval forces, Air Chief Marshal Leigh-Mallory Commander-in-Chief Allied Expeditionary Air Force, and General Spaatz, Commander United States Air Force in Europe. General Montgomery is not attending, he assures me he's ready to go, whatever the weather.

IKE gets out a cigarette and is about to light it.

LEIGH-MALLORY. Ike?

The cigarette sits unlit in IKE's *mouth.*

It's so difficult to concentrate in a room full of smoke.

IKE. For you, Trafford, we'll open the windows.

LEIGH-MALLORY. Cigarettes destroy one's mental acuity.

SPAATZ *flings open the French windows, then paces impatiently at the back of the room.*

BERTIE RAMSAY (*to* STAGG). Did you get the equipment you needed?

STAGG. Most of it, yes, sir.

BERTIE RAMSAY. You could always use one of my forecast rooms. If you don't think this room is suitable.

IKE. No he couldn't.

Outside, the familiar sound of a Spitfire overhead.

I want Stagg right here. Give him everything he wants, Bertie, but he stays here.

BERTIE RAMSAY (*looking out of the French windows*). It is an enviable view.

KAY *has walked in with a tray of coffee.*

STAGG. These...

He coughs to clear his throat. His voice trembles.

These are copies of my – (*Coughing again.*) my forecast.

STAGG *hands out the copies of the forecast.* SPAATZ *looks at his copy of the forecast vaguely, but seems uninterested.*

KAY *puts down the tray of coffee and starts to leave.*

IKE. Lieutenant Summersby, where you going? Stay. Keep the coffee flowing.

This familiarity, intimacy, does not go unnoticed.

SPAATZ. Ike, you know I'd trust Kay Summersby with my life, but is it appropriate she stays?

IKE. Goddamn right it is. I've given up keeping secrets from Kay. Anybody want sugar?

LEIGH-MALLORY (*raising a hand*). Two.

IKE. Okay, Stagg, what have you got for us?

The SECRETARY *opens her notebook, ready to take shorthand.*

SPAATZ. Where's Krick?

STAGG (*hesitating*)....He's not attending, sir.

SPAATZ. Why the hell not?

STAGG. I represent the Allied Meteorological Unit.

SPAATZ. Dr Stagg, I'm in command of over five thousand American aircraft. I've worked with Irving Krick since July '42. I wouldn't contemplate making a strategic choice without hearing his view. I want him here.

IKE. In future I'd like you both to be present. Okay, what have you got?

STAGG *turns to the chart.*

STAGG. We are faced with four...

The SECRETARY *starts writing. She looks up at* STAGG *as he hesitates.*

We are faced with four...

SPAATZ. Speak up.

STAGG....four, soon to be five, storms in the Atlantic of unprecedented intensity for the time of the year. Although... (*Clearing his throat again.*) there exists the seductive notion that this ridge of high pressure over the Azores could extend and deflect the storms, the Allied Meteorological Unit does not believe this is likely.

SPAATZ. 'Allied'? That include Irving Krick? What does he think?

STAGG. Colonel Krick and I have discussed this in considerable detail and these are the conclusions of the AMU.

SPAATZ. Okay, I'll take your word for it.

SPAATZ *looks sceptical, but* STAGG *battles on.*

STAGG. My forecast, therefore, for Monday 5th June, the proposed D-Day, is as follows: Wind: west-north-west. Strong. Reaching force five to six, possibly force seven.

BERTIE RAMSAY (*shocked*). Seven? Are you sure?

STAGG. That is my estimate.

BERTIE RAMSAY. Throughout the day?

STAGG. It's more than likely. Cloud: Low. Base 500 to 1000 feet. 7 to 9 10ths cover. Visibility: Poor. Rain: Very likely. The sea: Waves 6 feet to 10 feet, possibly increasing to 12 feet. Swell: Height 10 feet, wave length 750 feet. Confidence: Poor, falling to very poor through Monday 5th to Tuesday 6th.

STAGG *looks up. The Commanders-in-Chief are gloomy to a man.*

SPAATZ. Jesus Christ! 6 foot 1 of Stagg. 6 foot 2 of gloom.

And as if to mock everything STAGG *is suggesting, the sun dips lower outside, allowing a serene, golden light to pour into the room.*

I'm not a weatherman, Dr Stagg, but you expect me to believe your forecast? Look out the window, for God's sake!

STAGG. As I'm sure you know, sir, the weather in this part of the world can change very rapidly.

SPAATZ. It's been like this for six weeks, I'm sure it'll last another three days.

STAGG. I wish that were the case, sir.

BERTIE RAMSAY (*to* STAGG). Will the force-six winds continue through Tuesday and Wednesday?

STAGG. Any forecast beyond twenty-four to thirty-six hours is an informed guess...

IKE. Not according to Colonel Krick.

STAGG. No. Colonel Krick is enviably... certain. If I had to guess, I would say 'yes'. The force-six winds will probably continue through Tuesday and Wednesday.

BERTIE RAMSAY. You say 'poor visibility', how poor?

STAGG. Less than a mile.

LEIGH-MALLORY. What will conditions be like for my heavy bombers taking off early on Monday morning?

STAGG. 7 to 8 10ths stratus cloud. At 3,000 feet – thick. As I said, base 500 to 1000 feet.

LEIGH-MALLORY. And above the stratus?

STAGG. Considerable cloud between 8 and 12,000 feet.

LEIGH-MALLORY. What will the enemy have for their aircraft?

STAGG. Inland over France, weather will be better than over England. But on the coast – much the same as us.

Silence.

IKE. Thank you, Stagg. Tooey?

SPAATZ. We should 'go' regardless. The lives we'll save by shortening the war, will far outnumber the lives lost on D-Day. If we sit on our asses on this side of the Channel, the war could go on another five years. Get the men onto the beaches, somehow. Anyhow.

BERTIE RAMSAY (*a dose of reality*). General Spaatz, I can't land one hundred and sixty thousand men in a force-seven gale.

SPAATZ *has to concede this is true.* IKE *has had enough of not smoking. He takes out a Chesterfield, lights it and blows smoke into the air.*

Scene Two

5.00 p.m. Friday, 2 June 1944.

The room has emptied. STAGG looks pale and exhausted. He is slumped in a chair, holding the photograph of the pregnant woman and child. That's how KAY finds him when she returns to collect the empty coffee cups.

KAY (*encouraging*). All right, sir?

STAGG. Aye, I'm fine.

KAY (*brightly*). Coffee cups.

STAGG. Aye.

KAY starts to clear up the cups.

KAY. You look as if you've seen a ghost.

STAGG. I'm fine.

KAY. Is that your wife?

STAGG. Aye.

He's about to put the photo back on the table.

KAY. May I see?

A beat, then STAGG hands her the photo.

Is that your daughter?

STAGG. Son.

KAY. Oh, I'm sorry.

STAGG. He needed a haircut.

KAY. How old is he?

STAGG. Four.

The phone rings. STAGG picks it up.

Stagg...

He listens attentively and jots down some figures.

Thank you.

He puts down the phone, goes to the chart and makes an adjustment.

KAY. Your wife… is she…?

STAGG. Eight months pregnant. She had our son, Peter, early. So it could be any day.

KAY *picks up the note of anxiety in* STAGG*'s voice. She smiles at the photo.*

KAY. It's a lovely photograph.

STAGG. Could you put it back on the table.

KAY *replaces the photo. Silence.* STAGG *works on the chart, then asks a question which takes* KAY *by surprise.*

Do you have children?

KAY (*never self-pitying*). No! Not me! The war rather got in the way. I'm not even married. It would have been nice. Too late now.

STAGG. Is it? Why?

KAY. Various reasons. (*American accent.*) 'Not a problem' – as the Americans would say.

STAGG. You're young, fine looking, plenty of time.

KAY *is astonished by the compliment.* STAGG *continues to work.*

KAY. What's your wife's name?

STAGG. Elizabeth.

KAY. She'll be fine, Dr Stagg.

STAGG. There's no certainty of that. Childbirth doesn't agree with her.

STAGG *picks up a wooden louvered box, one of the instruments brought in by* ANDREW.

I'm going to set this up. In the grounds.

KAY. What is it?

STAGG. A Stevenson screen. Keeps instruments dry, keeps the air circulating.

He walks to the door, then stops.

What if Krick's right? What if summer's here to stay?

KAY. That would be good, wouldn't it?

STAGG *nods slowly, then leaves the room.* KAY *walks out onto the balcony, untucks her blouse and flaps it to cool down her body. She lifts her face to the sun, closes her eyes and feels the heat on her eyelids.*

She doesn't hear IKE *open the door. He stands in the open doorway watching her.*

Eventually, KAY *senses his presence and turns to face him.*

IKE. I didn't know England ever got this hot.

KAY *tucks in her blouse.*

Where's Stagg?

KAY. Setting up equipment in the grounds.

IKE *closes the door. He takes a key out of his pocket and locks the door.*

IKE. Five minutes.

KAY. Five whole minutes.

They stand, eyes locked, on opposite sides of the room.

You look so tired.

IKE. We're all tired. Even your uniform looks tired. Would you like a new one?

KAY. Yes please!

IKE. Soon as we get to Paris, we'll have one made.

KAY*'s face lights up.*

KAY. Paris! Imagine us in Paris.

Short silence. The sound of a ship's hooter from the harbour below. IKE *walks over to the chart.*

IKE. Do you understand it?

KAY (*joining* IKE *in front of the chart*). Not really, do you?

IKE. I'd like to, I'd really like to.

They stand side by side, a few feet apart, staring at the chart.

If Stagg's right, the landing craft will capsize. Fifty, sixty, seventy thousand men will drown before they even get to the beaches. Not exaggerating, Kay, these are fair-weather vessels, they don't even have a keel, for God's sake, some of them are twenty years old. If the cloud is low, the airborne won't know where to land, bombers won't see their targets, civilians will be killed. The weather has got to be good... And we have no back-up.

I don't know if it's positive thinking or foolishness, but we have no Plan B.

Another silence. KAY *pulls a chair over to* IKE.

KAY. Sit.

IKE *is obedient and sits.*

How is your knee?

IKE (*shrugging*). It's just a knee.

KAY *pulls another chair over and places it beside* IKE*'s. She sits next to him.* IKE *checks his watch.*

KAY. How long?

IKE. Three minutes.

Their hands hang loosely between the two chairs. They sit in silence for a moment, then almost tentatively, IKE *takes* KAY*'s hand. They sit in silence for a moment.*

I have a surprise for us. As rare as nylons.

IKE *reaches into his pocket and takes out… an orange.*

KAY. An orange! How smashing!!

She takes it from IKE *and smells it.*

Mmmmmmm! Where did you get it?

IKE. A secret admirer.

KAY. You can have as many admirers as you like if they bring
you oranges.

KAY *starts to peel the orange. Silence, then* IKE *continues
to unburden himself of the day's problems.*

IKE. Rommel… has doubled his beach defences in
Normandy… Why now? Why not in Calais? Why the
specific stretch of sand where we want to land? It cannot be a
coincidence. He knows, Kay. (*Needing an answer.*) Do you
think they're waiting for us?

KAY. Do you?

Silence. Eventually:

IKE (*truthful*). I don't know. I really don't know. Sixteen
months we've kept this secret. Jesus Christ!

KAY *has peeled the orange. Her hands are covered in juice.
She holds up a large segment in front of* IKE*'s mouth.* IKE
opens his mouth. KAY *pops the segment in. She pops one
into her own mouth too.*

Christ on the mountain, that is… so…

KAY. Mmmmmmmmm! Mmm! Mmm!

IKE. Delicious! Oh, wow!

KAY. That is the best… orange… I have ever…

*She feeds them both another segment – and another. They eat
in silence for a while, relishing the heavenly taste.*

IKE. We need a full moon, and dry beaches at low tide for half
an hour after touchdown. Those conditions only exist on the

5th. I can't bring D-Day forward, I can't delay it, and Stagg tells me we should expect force-seven gales on Monday. We're trapped. Jesus Christ, when did a coach ever rely on one play to win a match?

KAY *hands* IKE *a handkerchief. He wipes orange juice off his chin.*

The ship's hooter sounds again. A solitary aircraft passes overhead.

And Winston wants to watch the invasion from *HMS Belfast*.

KAY. Really?

IKE. Can you believe that? I said to him, 'I cannot sanction you taking that risk.' He said, 'As a Minister of Defence I have a duty to take part.' 'Bullshit'! I said. He said, 'I will circumvent your authority and go as a crew member.' Winston Churchill! A member of the crew?! 'Goddammit!' I said, 'It's D-Day minus three, haven't I got enough on my plate without having to worry about the Prime Minister's safety?'

KAY. What will you do?

IKE. Done it. I mentioned Winston's plan to the King.

KAY. What did he say?

IKE. The King sent a handwritten letter from Buckingham Palace to Ten Downing Street, saying that of course, as King, he would never interfere in the affairs of the Prime Minister, however, should the PM carry out his intentions, then as King, he would likewise feel obliged to witness the invasion as titular head of Britain's armed forces.

KAY. You are very brilliant!

IKE. Winston read the letter and told me he was bitterly disappointed and resentful. He said to me: 'If I do defer, which I assure you is by no means certain, I will be deferring to the Crown, not to you, General Eisenhower.'

KAY. He won't go. He can't risk the King's life.

IKE *looks at his watch.*

IKE. Time's up. More than up.

IKE *gets up. His knee gives way for a step or two towards the door, but then recovers. He unlocks the door and pockets the key. His hand is on the doorknob, he's about to leave, but he stops. Throughout the next speech he's facing the door, not* KAY.

(*Difficult to say, hesitant.*) Kay…

I don't know what I'd do without you… truly I don't… you work… so hard… you are so… special to me… if we win this war… and History gives me some of the credit… it will be in no small measure down to you.

IKE *opens the door and leaves. The tears well up in* KAY*'s eyes. She looks around for something to do. She pushes the two chairs back against a wall. Then she takes down* IKE*'s pile of correspondence. On top of the pile is a parcel.*

She sits at a table and unwraps the parcel. It contains a letter to Eisenhower, half a dozen eggs and a pair of sunglasses. She laughs, wiping away her tears. She puts on the shades. They rather suit her. She opens the egg box and smells them.

KAY. Oh God!

She pushes the eggs away in disgust. Clearly they're off.

The door opens. STAGG *returns.* KAY *is still wearing the sunglasses.* STAGG *stares at her. She suddenly realises and removes them.*

As if to explain her behaviour, KAY *reads the letter enclosed in* IKE*'s parcel.*

(*Reading.*) 'Dear General Eisenhower, my son Frank swears by Ray-Ban Aviator sunglasses, so I'm sending you a pair to protect you from the glare…

KAY *looks up at* STAGG, *then goes back to the letter.*

I enclose half a dozen fresh eggs…'

KAY *interjects:*

They are *not* fresh!

She continues reading:

'…please keep an eye on Frank for me. I know he admires you greatly. Yours respectfully, Mary Jane Palmer.'

KAY *puts down the letter.* STAGG *and* KAY *look at each other in silence. The silence is broken by one of the phones ringing.* STAGG *picks it up.*

STAGG. Yes… yes… one moment…

STAGG *mimes to* KAY *to take dictation from him.* KAY *finds paper and pencil.*

(*Dictating.*) 42.3 north. 15.4 west.

Pressure sea level: 1029 millibars.

KAY. M?

STAGG. M for… Methuselah.

KAY (*a glimmer of a smile*). Methuselah?

STAGG. Barometric change: plus 10.

Tendency: Rising.

Wind Speed: 3 knots.

Direction: South-west.

Temperature: 78 degrees.

(*Into phone.*) Thank you.

STAGG *puts down the phone.* KAY *gives him the dictated information.* STAGG *reads it, takes a red crayon and goes to the weather chart.*

He adjusts the curve of an isobar on the map north-east of the Azores. He draws a new red curve (visible to the audience) which stretches further to the north-east, towards the English Channel.

KAY. What do the figures mean?

STAGG *doesn't answer.*

Can you explain the figures to me?

Still no answer. STAGG *concentrates on the chart.*

Dr Stagg! I suspect you don't have much time for the English, but I'm not English, I'm Irish. We're both Celts, so don't take your prejudice out on me.

STAGG. I'm not in the slightest bit prejudiced.

STAGG *is still looking at the map.*

KAY. What does the red curve mean?

STAGG *answers* KAY*'s original question.*

STAGG. We have a British weather ship north-east of the Azores. This is their latest reading. All the thin lines are isobars. Measurements of barometric pressure.

STAGG *points to the barometer on the wall.*

No different from that barometer on the wall. The red curve is Colonel Krick's finger of high pressure pushing north-eastward towards the English Channel… as he predicted.

KAY. So the weather will be good on Monday?

STAGG. I don't believe so. You can never be certain, but I don't believe he's right. It does surprise me that the curve is so pronounced.

Suddenly the door is flung open. IKE *is in the room. He slams the door closed. His face is beetroot red, the veins stand out on his forehead. This is the legendary Eisenhower temper.*

IKE. Stagg, what in hell is going on?! Jesus H Christ! I wanna know now. Was the forecast you gave us the view of American *and* British forecasters?

STAGG *is silent.* IKE *is striding round the room, limping heavily.*

Answer the goddamn question!

STAGG. It was the view of the Allied Meteorological Unit.

IKE. Don't play games with me, you son-of-a-bitch! Because I've just had Spaatz on the telephone telling me that Krick's team think it's gonna be a beautiful, fucking summmer's day on Monday.

STAGG. Colonel Krick had no right to divulge…

IKE. He had every right to confer with his superior officer if he thought it would affect the outcome of the invasion.

The NAVAL METEOROLOGIST *appears in the doorway.*

Not now, goddammit!

The METEOROLOGIST *looks uncertain…*

Get out!!

NAVAL METEOROLOGIST. Sir.

The METEOROLOGIST *hurries out.*

STAGG. If you feel you can put greater trust in Colonel Krick…

IKE. You think I'm a goddamn child, Stagg?

STAGG. I didn't think uncertainty would be useful.

IKE. Jesus Christ, you listen to me. Over the last two years Krick has saved thousands of lives because of his forecasts. Again and again he gets it right. Why do you think he's wrong now?

STAGG *is silent.*

Listen, fella, you are gonna explain to me what that goddamn chart means and why I should trust you and not one of the unsung American heroes of this war. Why is Krick wrong?

No answer.

Why!

STAGG. I respect Colonel Krick as a scientist…

IKE. Answer the fucking question!

STAGG *hesitates, then:*

STAGG. Colonel Krick... has been lucky.

IKE. Good, I like luck, don't you? Why lucky?

STAGG (*nervous but strong*). Lucky because the weather systems when he made his forecasts were stable, so his analogous charts fitted conveniently. When patterns are predictable, charts from the past can be useful.

IKE. Goddamn right they're useful. In North Africa, he never made a mistake.

STAGG. Of course he didn't. He only forecasts if he's absolutely certain and in Morocco and Algeria in the summer, he was as safe as houses. This is northern Europe sir. Look at the chart: one, two, three, four, five storms which could, at any moment, erupt into terrible violence over the British Isles.

IKE (*pointing at the chart*). Why is that curve red?

STAGG. It's a more recent reading.

IKE. What does it mean?

STAGG. It means...

STAGG *trails off.* IKE *pounces.*

IKE. I can't hear ya, soldier.

STAGG. It means that high pressure from the Azores is pushing north-eastwards.

IKE. As Colonel Krick predicted it would. High pressure means good weather? Right?

STAGG. Usually. Not always.

IKE. In this case?

STAGG. The weather within the red curve would be calm, yes.

The phone rings. STAGG *lets it ring.*

IKE. Go ahead, answer it.

STAGG (*answering the phone*). Stagg… thank you…

He picks up a pen and jots down a message.

46.5 north. 12.3 west… 1028… thank you.

He puts down the phone.

IKE. Interesting?

STAGG. I'll adjust it later.

IKE. Do it now, I'm fascinated.

STAGG freezes.

(*Steely.*) Do it – *now*.

STAGG takes his red crayon to the chart. His back hides what he's drawing. When he's finished, he steps away. A second red curve of high pressure, i.e. calm weather, stretches from the Azores even further north-east. Even nearer the English Channel.

Krick's good weather is on the move. Am I right?

STAGG. Weather is always on the move.

IKE. And moving in the right direction, as he predicted.

STAGG. These are readings from one weather ship. Because of stormy seas, new readings from the Atlantic will take longer to come through.

IKE. When's the next chart due?

STAGG. One o'clock, tomorrow morning.

IKE. That should clarify things?

STAGG. I hope so.

IKE. One of you is right.

STAGG. Yes, sir.

IKE. Before this game kicked off, it was decided the Chief Meteorological Officer should be British.

STAGG. So your hands are tied?

IKE. There's no question of Krick taking over, but you know as well as I do that Allied unity is essential.

Short silence. IKE *walks to the chart and stares at the mass of curves, lines and figures.*

STAGG. Sir…

IKE *turns back to* STAGG.

British weather is uniquely complex and erratic.

IKE. I wouldn't want to book a holiday in advance.

STAGG. I lived for two years on a weather ship off the west coast of Scotland. I witnessed winds of one hundred and thirty miles per hour, summer temperatures of ninety degrees, I measured a wave of sixty feet between the Isle of Arran and the Ayrshire coast. It's a climate of surprises… of twists and turns… you have to sense the rise and fall on the hall barometer before the arrow even moves. It's a science governed by instinct and experience as much as formulae. You'll have to trust that my instincts are good.

Silence.

IKE. You know Ayrshire well?

STAGG. I do.

IKE. You know Culzean Castle?

STAGG. Very well.

IKE. You ever watched the geese flying in from the west?

STAGG. Often.

IKE. What a sound. Primeval. Fundamental.

STAGG. It's a sound I'd welcome on my deathbed. Geese will tell you as much as a barometer. 'When the geese pass over Kintyre, bring in the peats, stock up the fire.'

Long moment. IKE *walks up close to* STAGG.

IKE. If there is divergence, I want to know. Is that clear?

STAGG *doesn't answer.*

(*Frightening intensity.*) Is – that – clear?

Dr Stagg?

STAGG. Aye, it is.

IKE *turns to* KAY *and notices she is still holding the sunglasses.*

IKE. Where d'you get those?

KAY *is momentarily confused, but then clicks.*

KAY. Oh, these are for you. Sent by a Mrs Palmer to protect you from the glare.

IKE *takes the shades and tries them on.*

IKE. What do you think?

KAY. Um. They rather blot you out.

IKE. Christ on the mountain, I don't want to be blotted out. Is that your impression, Dr Stagg?

STAGG. Al Capone springs to mind.

IKE. Now that I like. Strike some fear into those Nazi bastards.

IKE *takes off the sunglasses and clips them onto his breast pocket.*

Please tell Mrs Palmer how useful they will be in the glare of a French summer.

And he leaves. Silence. STAGG *thinking,* KAY *watching* STAGG. *A phone rings.* STAGG *answers it.*

STAGG (*on phone*)….Stagg… Yes…

A second phone rings.

50.5 north…

STAGG *gestures to* KAY. *She grabs paper and pencil and answers the second phone.*

KAY (*on phone*). Lieutenant Summersby… yes… yes…

STAGG (*on phone*).…32.7 west…

KAY (*on phone*). I'll pass that on to him…

STAGG *glances at* KAY, *a flicker of interest, nothing more.*

STAGG (*on phone*). 1016…

KAY (*on phone*). No.

STAGG (*on phone*). 1010…

KAY (*on phone*). Dr Forbes?…

For STAGG, *the name of the doctor is like an electric shock.
His attention instantly switches to* KAY's *call. He gestures to
her, mouthing the words: 'I want to speak to him.'*

Yes I will… yes… yes…

STAGG *realises he hasn't heard his caller's last figures.*

STAGG (*on phone*). I beg your pardon, could you repeat that…

KAY (*on phone*). Where is she…?

STAGG (*on phone*). 2 knots…

KAY (*on phone*). I see. Can we contact her?…

STAGG (*on phone*). 2 knots rising… aye…

KAY (*on phone*). That seems excessive…

STAGG (*on phone*). I'm sorry, could you… repeat… 4 knots,
thank you…

STAGG *struggles to focus on his call. He looks pale,
frightened.*

KAY (*on phone*). Surely you can give me a telephone number?…

STAGG (*on phone*). 998…

KAY (*on phone*). It's a hospital, not Ten Downing Street!

STAGG (*on phone*). 1001, aye…

KAY (*on phone*). Well, please let us know, as soon as you hear anything… I'd be grateful…

STAGG *gesticulates for* KAY *to keep the call going – too late.*

Thank you… goodbye.

She puts the phone down, STAGG*'s call trickles on.* KAY *waits for it to end.*

STAGG (*on phone*). North-north-east… 3 knots… 1010, east-south-east 2 knots rising… thank you. Goodbye.

STAGG *is repeating the figures but failing to write them down. The call ends. He looks at* KAY *desperately.*

KAY. Your wife left a message with the Met Office in London… Your baby's on the way.

STAGG. I knew this would happen.

KAY. She's on her way to hospital.

STAGG. Which one?

KAY. Southampton General.

STAGG (*extremely anxious*). I need to talk to her. Did they give you a contact number?

KAY. I'm afraid 'security' blocked it.

STAGG. I need to see her.

KAY. She'll be in safe hands.

STAGG. What did they say about Dr Forbes?

KAY. He's been informed.

STAGG. I need to speak to him, there must be a way of contacting the hospital, I may have his telephone number.

He hurries to his suitcase and opens it.

KAY. You won't be able to call him, Dr Stagg.

STAGG *is rummaging through his case.*

Trunk calls are forbidden. They're going to leave a message with the Met Office as soon as there are any developments.

STAGG. Dr Forbes has all the information about our son Peter's birth… it was not straightforward… not at all straightforward … did they say how long Liz had been in labour?

KAY. She'll be fine.

STAGG. You know *nothing* about it! There is no certainty she will be fine, none whatsoever!

STAGG looks distraught. The phone rings again. STAGG *appears paralysed.* KAY *has to answer it.*

KAY (*on phone*). Thank you… 54.2 north… 28.6 west… 1014…

The NAVAL METEOROLOGIST *enters. He holds out papers for* STAGG.

NAVAL METEOROLOGIST. New signals from *How*, sir.

STAGG looks at the METEOROLOGIST *blankly, as… a second phone rings. It rings insistently.* KAY *covers her receiver with her hand.*

KAY. Dr Stagg!

Eventually, STAGG *picks up the phone, his hand is trembling. The following dialogue overlaps.*

STAGG (*on phone*). Stagg…

KAY. Rising …

STAGG. 44.3 north…

KAY. South-west-south…

The NAVAL METEOROLOGIST *places the papers on* STAGG's *table, as the third phone rings.*

STAGG. 18.5 west…

KAY. 3 knots…

KAY *points at the third phone. The* METEOROLOGIST *picks up the phone.*

STAGG. 1016…

KAY. Drizzle and fog…

NAVAL METEOROLOGIST (*on phone*). This is Group Captain Stagg's Office…

STAGG. West-south-west 3 knots…

KAY. Visibility, poor…

STAGG. Visibility, good…

The phone calls continue as the lights fade.

Scene Three

Nine hours later. 3.00 a.m. Saturday, 3 June 1944.

Two desk lamps light the room. Shutters in front of the French windows have been closed. The blackout is in place.

The bombers we heard in the first scene are returning from their mission. Not a concerted roar now, but planes flying home individually, intermittently.

KRICK *is immersed in his analogue charts. Tie loosened. Tired.* STAGG *and* ANDREW *are in front of the chart, exhausted, but checking a new set of readings.* ANDREW *reads,* STAGG *adjusts the chart, which is now a mass of red curves, crosses and scribbled numbers as the weather evolves.*

STAGG *is controlled but distracted.*

ANDREW. 50.6, 35.1 – 1006…

STAGG. 1006.

ANDREW. 44.3, 38.2…

STAGG. Aye.

ANDREW. 1009…

STAGG *loses concentration.* ANDREW *has to repeat the number.*

Sir?

No response.

Sir?... 1009.

STAGG (*refocusing*). 1009. 38.2?

ANDREW. Yes, sir.

STAGG *makes another adjustment.* ANDREW *checks his watch.*

Three o'clock. Two hours late.

STAGG. Aye, not surprising.

ANDREW *is still looking at his watch.*

ANDREW. Fifty-one hours to go.

STAGG *gestures to* ANDREW*'s list of readings.*

STAGG. Next.

ANDREW. 44.2, 36.5.

A phone rings. ANDREW *moves to answer it, but* STAGG *stops him.*

STAGG. I'll take it.

He hurries to the phone, hoping for news from the hospital.

Hello... (*Deflated.*) Yes... yes... Thank you...

He puts down the phone.

Blacksod Point on the Irish coast has recorded a force-six wind. Their barometer is falling rapidly.

KRICK. Proves nothing.

STAGG (*a sudden explosion of anger*). It proves something, Colonel Krick! It absolutely proves something!

STAGG goes back to the chart and aggressively circles Blacksod Point. He scrawls an equation beside the circle: 'WI=5(HMxRQ)(G<2-30xQL-2QM).'

The door opens. KRICK, STAGG *and* ANDREW *turn hopefully, but it's not what they're expecting – it's* KAY, *dressed in a voluminous boiler suit, covered in oil. Her hair is roughly tied back. She's carrying a tray of coffee.*

KAY. Coffee?

KRICK. Wonderful girl! You know your way to a man's heart.

KAY puts down the tray.

KAY. Black or white?

KRICK. Black, sweetheart.

KAY. I warn you it's a powerful brew. Ike won't have coffee that isn't scalding hot and black as molasses. (*To* STAGG.) No sign?

STAGG is studying the chart, unravelling his equation, he appears not to hear. ANDREW *answers for him.*

ANDREW. We may have to postpone the meeting.

KRICK (*to* KAY). Where the hell did you get those overalls?

KRICK takes a fold of KAY's boiler suit between his fingers.

This is soft!

KAY. Brushed cotton. This, I'll have you know, is one of the Prime Minister's cast-offs!

KRICK. Are you serious?

KAY. Absolutely serious.

She holds out the sides of the boiler suit, she looks as if she's sprouted wings.

He's a little wider of course.

ANDREW (*star-struck*). Is it really one of Churchill's?

KAY. For some reason, Ike always plonks me next to the PM when he comes to dinner. Milk, Dr Stagg?

STAGG *is absorbed in the chart.*

Dr Stagg?

ANDREW *answers for* STAGG.

ANDREW. A little.

KAY. We were talking cars, he said he had just the thing for me. D'you see the burn mark under the breast pocket? He fell asleep and dropped his cigar, when he woke up he was practically on fire!

KAY *checks her watch. She tries to draw* STAGG *into the conversation.*

(*To* STAGG.) The chart's two hours late.

STAGG. Conditions in the Atlantic are appalling.

KRICK. Difficult for the weather ships to get information out.

KAY (*to* STAGG). Do you want me to delay General Eisenhower?

STAGG. Give it a few more minutes.

KRICK. You been working on the car tonight?

KAY. I do most of my work on the car at night. The garage has no windows, so I can turn on the lights. It's rather peaceful.

KRICK (*tasting the coffee*). My God, this'd blow your head off. More brake problems?

KAY. No, I was replacing the fuel pump. As you can see.

She holds up her hands which are even oilier than usual. Short silence, just the surreal sound of the cups clinking, as they stand there in the dim light, sipping their coffee.

A different sound draws their attention to the balcony. Another bomber is returning home, but the engine sounds fitful, erratic, occasionally it appears to cut out altogether.

STAGG. He's in trouble.

STAGG goes to the French windows.

Lights.

ANDREW *and* KAY *switch off the desk lamps.*

Pitch black. STAGG *opens the shutters.*

His wing's on fire.

KAY, ANDREW *and* KRICK *join him. They all look out.*

KAY. Oh my God.

KRICK. Jesus Christ, they're not going to make it.

As if on cue, the bomber's engine stutters again. The sound changes to a 'scream' as the plane starts to fall out of the sky. The scream of the engine gets louder and louder. Then, there's an eerie silence for about ten seconds, followed by a huge explosion. The night sky turns red. The forecasters and KAY*'s faces are lit up.*

Jesus Christ.

KAY. Did you see if anyone got out?

ANDREW. It's dark, we wouldn't necessarily see them.

KRICK. They may have bailed out a while ago.

ANDREW. Do you think they crashed in Portsmouth?

KAY. I think they missed the town... thank God.

The light continues to flicker on their faces as they watch the blaze in silence. Fire-engine bells ring. The sound of people shouting.

A knock on the door breaks the mood.

STAGG (*to the person knocking*). Wait! One moment!

Quickly, efficiently, they close the shutters and switch on the lamps, re-establishing the blackout.

Come!

The door opens. The NAVAL METEOROLOGIST *enters carrying the next rolled-up weather chart. This is what they've been waiting for.*

NAVAL METEOROLOGIST. Synoptic chart, sir. 0100 GMT. Sorry about the delay, sir.

STAGG *takes the chart. The* METEOROLOGIST *leaves.*

STAGG (*to* ANDREW). Give me a hand.

STAGG *climbs one set of library steps.*

ANDREW *climbs the other.* ANDREW *holds the chart steady as* STAGG *pins it. Huge anticipation.*

STAGG *and* ANDREW *let go of the chart. It rolls down over the previous chart. There is a new caption at the top: '0100 GMT SATURDAY JUNE 3. 1944.'*

STAGG *and* ANDREW *climb down.*

KRICK *and* STAGG *go to work.*

Andrew, I'll need the freezing level at Valentia and lapse rate at Blacksod.

ANDREW *scribbles some calculations.*

At lightning speed, KRICK *writes an equation on his side of the chart: '$1012=1/6 \times 1012(1012-1)(1012-2)$'*

STAGG *writes one on his side: '$Q=(WBC+273.15)(1000/Mb)<0.286+(3m)$'*

STAGG *turns to* KRICK.

Surely, surely now you can not contend that the Channel will escape stormy weather?

KRICK *looks at* STAGG *in utter amazement.*

KRICK. You've gotta be kidding? You have *got* to be kidding.

STAGG. Of course I'm not.

KRICK. Goddammit! Look at the high pressure from the Azores, it's already here!

STAGG. Yes, briefly.

KRICK. 1017 in East Anglia, 1020 in Devon...

STAGG. I can read.

KRICK. 1023 in Biscay, 1026 off the north coast of Spain.

STAGG. I see that.

KRICK. You need more proof?

STAGG. It proves nothing. Look at this! 3 and 5 have merged to form a lethal new entity L6. Look at the pressure gradient: '02, '05, '08.

STAGG circles L6 in frustration.

Your anti-cyclone will be helpless.

KRICK. Bullshit!

STAGG. You heard the readings from Blacksod, the barometric pressure is hurtling down.

KRICK. It's not fucking hurtling!

STAGG. '17 to '14 in three hours.

KRICK. And that's as low as it's going to get, buddy. Listen, I'm going to try to stay calm here...

The next speeches could be overlapped, as the men try to force their opinions home.

Pressure has risen from East Anglia to Barcelona...

STAGG....upper-air currents have strengthened around the north of the British Isles...

KRICK....L3 is filling up...

STAGG....cold air is pouring south...

KRICK....moist westerly winds...

STAGG....vigorous depressions will be forced eastwards...

KRICK....will affect *only* the central...

STAGG.…their associated troughs…

KRICK.…and northern parts of the British Isles.

STAGG (*almost screaming it out*). ARE BOUND TO AFFECT
THE CHANNEL ADVERSELY!!

KRICK. You know what, I can't stand your Scotch pessimism
any more, your Highland gloom.

STAGG. I'm not from the Highlands.

KRICK. Well, your fucking Lowland gloom then.

STAGG. I am neither from the Highlands nor the Lowlands!

KRICK. Goddammit, we should have left you to the Germans,
you're not worth saving.

*The two men run out of words. They stare at each other
furiously.*

A phone rings in the silence. ANDREW *answers it. He holds
out the receiver to* STAGG.

ANDREW. Sir?

STAGG *takes the phone.*

STAGG (*on phone*). Yes… this is Dr Stagg… aye…

The colour drains from STAGG*'s face.*

(*Extremely worried.*) Did they say why?…

The door opens and IKE *enters.*

KRICK *stands to attention and salutes* IKE. IKE *returns the
salute, then holds out his hand. They shake hands.*

IKE. How are you, Irving?

KRICK. Very good, sir. How are you?

IKE. A-one.

STAGG (*on phone, anxious*). When?… Can you tell me when
this was?

IKE. Is that coffee?

KAY *starts to pour* IKE *a cup.*

Is it hot?

KAY *stops pouring.*

Really hot?

KAY. I'll make some more.

KAY *leaves with the coffee pot.* IKE *focuses on* STAGG *for a moment.*

STAGG (*on phone*). That's all they said?... That can't be all they said!

IKE *turns back to* KRICK.

IKE. Where have they billeted you, Irv?

KRICK. I've got a neat little tent in the grounds.

IKE. Good. Did you bring a football?

KRICK. Always do.

IKE. Good man. There's a tennis court behind the house. If we get a moment, we'll throw some passes.

KRICK. I'd like that.

STAGG (*on phone*). Surely you can tell me when this was!... Well... could you... please let me know if you have any further information... Aye... I'd be grateful.

STAGG *puts down the phone.*

IKE. Something I should know about, Stagg?

STAGG. No, sir. Nothing of importance.

IKE. Okay, what have you got for me? Has the new chart brought you two guys together?

STAGG. No, sir.

IKE *looks at his watch.*

IKE. Listen to me. It's a quarter of three. In twenty-one hours I have to give the order for three thousand Naval vessels harboured around these islands to leave their ports and sail south. They're waiting in Belfast, Grimsby, Liverpool, Greenock and Scapa Flow. You gotta help me here, guys. Do I give the order to sail or not? Irving, would you give that order?

KRICK. I would, sir.

IKE. Why?

KRICK. I'm looking at a weather system over the Azores, an anti-cyclone of great calmness and stability pushing north towards the Channel – never felt so certain, never felt so justified in feeling positive and optimistic. We go back a few years, Ike, I've never let you down. Carpe diem, sir.

IKE. Stagg?

STAGG. Throughout this afternoon I've received measurements of upper-air currents at a range of altitudes. An unprecedented depth of information. All of the currents are moving abnormally rapidly. The jet stream has increased its speed to 140 knots. These upper winds will drive this massive storm L6 towards the British isles. I am in little doubt that it will pass through the English Channel on Monday 5th and persist into Tuesday the 6th.

IKE. So you're saying: don't give the order to sail?

STAGG. I'm saying… I'm saying that I believe the weather on D-Day will be extremely poor.

KAY *returns with a cup of scalding black coffee for* IKE. *She walks into the tensest of silences.* IKE *takes the coffee and goes to the chart.*

IKE. Even I can see Irving's anti-cyclone is on the move, Stagg.

STAGG. It is indeed.

IKE. This is not the moment for vanity on either of your parts. Is this a question of pride?

STAGG (*shocked*). Do you truly believe I would allow personal pride to get in the way of my objectivity as a scientist?

IKE. I don't believe you would, but I ask the question anyway.

STAGG (*heartfelt*). The question is too insulting to answer.

IKE. When do we get the next chart?

STAGG. Early afternoon.

IKE. So there is still time for the situation to resolve itself?

STAGG. The likelihood is that the situation will remain confused…

KRICK. Far as I'm concerned, there's no confusion, the situation is very clear.

STAGG (*to* IKE). You will have to make a choice. My feeling is you've already chosen.

IKE *looks at the chart seeking inspiration.*

IKE. At this moment in time… I see no reason to disbelieve Colonel Krick's prognosis. I know nothing, but your… theory, Irving… seems plausible. And there it is, on the map, I see the evidence…

He places his hands over the Azores.

I'm a layman, but I see, with my own eyes, the good weather moving north…

KRICK. As it did, identically, on three previous occasions this century, and on every occasion this pattern was followed by a period of calm weather in the English Channel.

IKE. You see my problem, Dr Stagg.

STAGG. I understand… how easy it is… to be deceived by this chart.

IKE. Okay. (*Thinking hard.*) Okay. Early afternoon we get a new chart. We'll meet again with the C-in-Cs. But I'm here to tell you, that'll be the last conceivable opportunity to change *anything*. We have to hope the next chart confirms your theory, Irving, but whether it does or doesn't I will have to make a decision. Is that clear?

IKE *walks to the door.*

Try to get some sleep, gentlemen.

IKE *leaves.*

KRICK. Okay, you heard the boss.

KRICK *tidies his table.*

I'm going to hunker down, get some shut-eye.

He drains his coffee.

Thanks for the coffee, sweetheart.

He goes to the door.

You know where to find me, Stagg. Come and get me if you need me. Goodnight.

And KRICK *leaves. Long silence.*

KAY (*carefully*). Who was on the telephone?

STAGG (*profoundly shaken*). The hospital is keeping my wife in overnight. Her blood pressure is high.

KAY. I see.

STAGG. This is exactly what happened before.

KAY. I don't know much about blood pressure.

STAGG. High blood pressure during pregnancy is extremely dangerous.

KAY. I didn't know.

STAGG. For the mother and the baby.

KAY. I see.

Silence. STAGG *in his own thoughts.*

Can it be lowered?

STAGG. There is a drug. Potassium Thiocyanate. Its
    effectiveness is unproven. The side effects are not good.

KAY. But it's the same doctor… who treated your wife last time?

STAGG. Dr Forbes.

KAY. The same hospital?

STAGG. Aye.

KAY. Well, perhaps the familiar surroundings…

STAGG. If the blood pressure remains high, their lives are in
    danger. That's the simple truth.

STAGG goes to the chart and stares again at his storms, at
    KRICK*'s anti-cyclone. He picks up a pen and is about to
    make another adjustment, but notices that his hand is
    trembling. He tries to write something on the chart, but he's
    shaking too much. He quickly lowers his hand.*

Long silence. STAGG *stands with his back to* KAY *and*
    ANDREW. *Eventually, he turns to them.*

General Eisenhower has made his choice.

KAY. But you don't believe Colonel Krick's theory, do you?

No response from STAGG.

Dr Stagg?

STAGG. It's plausible.

KAY. But you don't believe it.

ANDREW, *who has watched the previous scene, almost
    invisibly, suddenly speaks out.*

ANDREW. Miss Summersby, in my opinion, if General
    Eisenhower places his trust in Colonel Krick, he'll be
    making a terrible mistake.

Blackout.

Interval.

ACT TWO

Scene One

Two hours later. 5.00 a.m. Saturday, 3 June 1944.

The electric lights are off. The first grey dawn light is visible through cracks in the shutters.

STAGG *is scrunched up in a chair, trying to sleep. He is in his uniform, using his jacket as a pillow. His tie hangs from a nail on the wall. He shifts restlessly. He checks his watch. Sleep is impossible.*

He makes a decision. He stands up and buttons the collar of his shirt. He reaches for his tie. He loops it round his collar and begins to tie a knot. He appears calm, but his hands won't function. The knot is a failure. He pulls the tie apart and allows his hands to drop to his side. The tie lies unfastened round his neck.

He tries again, with more success, the knot is reasonable, the tie is on. He folds down his collar and straightens the tie. He puts his jacket on.

He picks up the photograph of his wife and takes it to his suitcase. He opens the case and places the photo inside. He closes the case, picks it up and walks towards the door. Halfway across the room, his courage fails. He puts down the case. He stands, motionless…

There is a soft knock on the door. KAY *pops her head round and sees* STAGG, *standing in the middle of the room, his suitcase packed. She enters the room quietly. She's carrying a cup of coffee.*

KAY. Good morning, sir.

STAGG. Good morning.

KAY. I brought you a cup of coffee.

STAGG. It's five o'clock in the morning.

KAY. I had a feeling you'd be up.

> KAY *assesses* STAGG. *She puts down the cup of coffee, opens the shutters and lets in the dawn light.* STAGG *hasn't moved.*

> Why don't you sit down, Dr Stagg?

> *No response.*

> Have a cup of coffee.

> *No response.*

> Come and sit down.

STAGG. I'm going to the hospital.

KAY. I see.

STAGG. I need to talk to Liz. I need to see her.

KAY. I understand.

STAGG. I need to talk to Dr Forbes.

KAY. Yes.

> STAGG *looks exhausted on his feet.*

> Do you plan to come back?

STAGG. It would be easier for General Eisenhower if I didn't.

KAY. How will you get there?

STAGG. You could drive me.

KAY. No.

STAGG. We could be at the hospital by eight.

KAY. No.

> *Silence.* STAGG *is still standing, motionless, beside his suitcase.*

> You'd be tried for desertion. You'd probably be shot.

STAGG. I'm the wrong man for the job. General Eisenhower has made his choice. Krick's thesis is perfectly plausible.

KAY. Except you don't believe it.

STAGG. I need to know… if she's alright.

KAY. I understand.

STAGG. We nearly lost Peter. Liz could have died.

Silence. Warily, KAY *tries again:*

KAY. Why don't you sit down, sir? (*A beat.*) Dr Stagg? Come and sit down.

Slowly KAY *walks over to* STAGG. *She takes his arm. He stiffens.*

Come on.

KAY *gently pulls his arm. Initially he resists, but eventually he allows* KAY *to lead him to a chair. He sits.*

KAY *watches him for a moment, then hands him his cup of coffee.*

Have a sip.

STAGG *manages to get the cup to his lips, but his hands start to tremble.* KAY *quickly rescues the cup of coffee. The trembling gets worse, it spreads through* STAGG's *body, until his entire frame is shaking. He's shaking so much, he finds it hard to breathe.*

KAY *places a hand on his shoulder. She waits. The trembling continues.*

Dr Stagg? Are you listening?

She waits, patiently.

Are you listening?

I can't drive you to the hospital, but there may be something I can do. I could go to Southampton, on my own. Are you listening? As you say, if I left now, I would be back in time for the meeting.

STAGG *takes this in*.

STAGG. I couldn't ask you to do that.

KAY. You wouldn't have to. I've volunteered.

STAGG. Why would you do that for me?

KAY. Because I suspect you know more about Monday's weather than Colonel Krick ever will. Let me go to Southampton. To the hospital. I'll visit your wife, talk to your doctor and report back to you. (*Gentle*.) Did you hear what I said?

STAGG. Aye.

The trembling gradually subsides. STAGG is left wrung out, utterly drained. With two hands he takes the cup of coffee and guides it to his lips. He takes a sip. He slumps back into his chair.

I couldn't sleep. Have you slept?

KAY. No. None of the family sleep much.

STAGG. Family?

KAY. Ike's family. The war family.

STAGG closes his eyes. He wants KAY to talk.

STAGG. Who's who? In the family?

KAY (*soothing*). Colonel Lee, have you met him?

STAGG shakes his head, eyes still closed.

We call him Tex.

They meet over breakfast, smoke Chesterfields, drink black coffee… organise the day.

STAGG (*murmured*). Tex.

KAY. Bedell Smith. Beetle. He's cooking Ike his scrambled eggs as we speak. And Mickey, who would die for Ike, is downstairs pressing his uniform. Me, of course, wide awake… and you, Dr Stagg, an honoury guest of the family, also wide awake.

KAY's speech has calmed STAGG.

STAGG. What's your role?

KAY. Oh, general dogsbody, me. Driver, secretary... mechanic! (*Heartfelt.*) I love driving. I've driven Ike for three years. Morocco, Algeria, Tunisia... we're onto our third car!

A short silence.

The family's been together since 1941. (*Unguarded.*) I've never been happier.

Another silence. Then with an assumed levity which fails to mask her sadness:

D-Day is the beginning of the end. I want you to stay, Dr Stagg, and help Ike make the right decision.

STAGG. He doesn't want to believe me.

KAY. No he doesn't.

Outside the French windows, early morning sun begins to break through the mist.

I'm going to say something which will seem cruel. I'm sure your wife is going to be just fine, but *whatever* happens to her, you must stay here. If staying here and sticking to your guns saves fifty thousand lives... it would be a terrible thing to leave us now.

STAGG *says nothing.*

So... I'll go to Southampton General Hospital and ask for Mrs Elizabeth Stagg?

STAGG *nods.*

I'll tell her you're well. And I'll see how she is. All right?

STAGG *nods.*

But first I have to persuade General Eisenhower. Go for a walk now. The fresh air will do you good. Don't come back for at least half an hour.

STAGG *doesn't move.*

Off you go.

STAGG. Now?

KAY nods.

Should I go now?

KAY. Yes please.

STAGG stands up, he feels weak and dizzy.

STAGG. Aye. I'll go for a walk.

He walks slowly to the door.

Thank you, Lieutenant Summersby.

KAY. Not at all.

STAGG leaves. KAY picks up one of the phones and dials an extension.

(*On phone.*) Have you started the meeting yet?… Could you give me two minutes?… I'm in Dr Stagg's office… I understand. Just two minutes… thank you.

She puts down the phone. She goes to the French windows and opens them. A tiny breeze flicks the muslin curtains, the first hint of wind since the play began.

KAY hears the click of the door. She turns. IKE is in the room. The first thing he does is check his watch.

IKE. This will have to be quick. I'm keeping people waiting.

KAY. Do you need me this morning?

IKE. I always need you.

KAY. I'd like to visit Dr Stagg's wife in hospital.

IKE. You're kidding.

KAY. The Liberty Bus to Southampton leaves… (*Checking her watch.*) in twenty minutes… full of Wrens going home from the night shift. No one would notice an extra passenger.

IKE. It's D-Day minus two.

KAY. I'd be back in time for the meeting with the C-in-Cs.

IKE (*simple, final*). No.

KAY. Why not?

IKE. Out of the question.

KAY. Please let me go.

IKE (*incredulous*). To visit Stagg's wife?

> KAY *looks at her watch. Precious minutes are ticking by.*

KAY. What do you think of Dr Stagg?

> IKE *moves as if to leave.*

Please! What do you think of him?

IKE. Scottish.

KAY. When I first met him, I thought he was insufferable...

> IKE *is losing patience.* KAY *battles on.*

But actually he's just direct.

> IKE *waits impatiently.*

I trust him, don't you?

> IKE *says nothing.*

If he believes something strongly, he'll say it because he believes it's the truth.

IKE. Sure, that's the problem.

KAY. I believe he knows more about British weather than Colonel Krick, don't you?

IKE. I'm not a meteorologist. Nor are you.

KAY. His wife is expecting their second child.

IKE. Okay, Kay, I'm in a meeting...

KAY. The Met Office rang to tell him she's been taken into Southampton Hospital...

IKE. Lieutenant Summersby...

KAY. The birth of Mrs Stagg's first child was not straightforward. Dr Stagg is understandably extremely anxious.

IKE. I don't give a damn if he's anxious, there are three hundred thousand men down there, willing to sacrifice their lives.

But KAY, *carefully, pursues her course.*

KAY. If I can get reassurance from Mrs Stagg, I believe he will be in a better state of mind to… focus, without distraction. Without that reassurance, I'm not… confident he will cope. He's under huge strain.

IKE *says nothing.* KAY *has no idea if he's listening or not.*

I've never asked you for anything. I've never asked for a day off. My friends all think I've given them up. Just this once… Ike? Would you do this for me? If Dr Stagg does his job better, it's worth it, isn't it? Less than forty-eight hours to go.

KAY *looks at her watch again, tears of frustration well up in her eyes.*

Please trust me. Please. (*Quiet.*) The bus leaves in fifteen minutes.

Silence, then:

I've sorted the morning out. It's all in the Blue Book. Working breakfast with Tex till 7.30. 8 till 10 with the PM. 10.15 Ramsay…

IKE (*interrupting*). Winston arrives at a quarter of eight. I want you here to mollify him.

KAY. Dr Stagg believes his wife and the baby are in danger.

IKE. No. That's final.

KAY *risks everything:*

KAY. You're a father. You lost a son.

Silence. IKE*'s face gives nothing away.*

Then:

IKE. You think it'll make a difference to Stagg's performance if you go?

KAY (*very simple, looking straight into* IKE*'s eyes*). Yes I do. I really do.

IKE looks at KAY steadily.

IKE. Orders are to shoot on sight anybody trying to leave the compound without identification. You'll need a travel pass. Get Tex to fix you up.

KAY (*heartfelt*). Thank you.

She reaches up and kisses him on the cheek. She hurries to the door.

IKE. Be careful.

KAY. I will.

IKE. Don't get yourself shot.

KAY. I'll be back for the meeting.

IKE. Kay.

KAY (*almost out of the room*). Yes.

IKE. I love you.

KAY (*still facing the door*). I love you too.

Blackout.

Scene Two

Eight hours later. 1.00 p.m. Saturday, 3 June 1944.

The scene begins at the exact moment that the crucial 1 p.m. chart unrolls.

IKE, LEIGH-MALLORY, RAMSAY *and* SPAATZ *watch as* STAGG *and* KRICK *examine the chart. Both men write out more equations and formulae.* STAGG *looks nervous. His hand trembles as he writes.*

A tiny breeze blows the muslin curtains inwards, but they settle again and it's as hot and still as ever.

STAGG (*to* KRICK). Do you have a pressure tendency at 54.2 north?

> KRICK *checks on his side of the chart.*

KRICK. 2 millibars in three hours.

STAGG. And at 58.6?

KRICK. The same.

STAGG. Thank you.

> STAGG *jots down the figures.*

KRICK (*to* STAGG). Confirm for me L8's central pressure?

STAGG. 996.

> *They continue in silence, then* STAGG *turns to the C-in-Cs.*

Gentlemen, one feature has changed substantially since the last chart. The long north-eastward extension of the Azores anti-cyclone has withdrawn from Ireland and been forced south into the Bay of Biscay.

We can no longer rely on this ridge of high pressure to offer any protection whatsoever to the English Channel on 5th June. Obviously I haven't conferred with Colonel Krick yet, but I imagine he would agree.

KRICK. No I would not.

STAGG *is stunned*.

STAGG. On what grounds?

KRICK. If you look at the charts of June 1923, you will see a similar, *temporary* weakening of the high pressure over the Azores. Within twenty-four hours it had reinforced itself and pushed north-eastward again.

STAGG. Not so in 1907, not so in 1915. You pick 1923 because it suits your purpose.

SPAATZ. Are you implying, Dr Stagg, that Colonel Krick is distorting the truth to persuade us?

STAGG. Not distorting the truth, no…

SPAATZ. I trust the Colonel's integrity – totally. I trust his record, which is second to none. Gentlemen, many of my men owe their lives to the accuracy of Colonel Krick's forecasts.

KRICK. This chart is exactly what I expected. I maintain my prediction of calm, sunny weather for Monday.

IKE. Your prediction, Dr Stagg?

STAGG. Force-six winds, low cloud…

LEIGH-MALLORY. How low?

STAGG. 500 feet. Considerable swell: waves of 10 to 12 feet, possibly 15 feet.

The Commanders-in-Chief are aware for the first time of the extent of divergence between the two forecasters.

LEIGH-MALLORY (*impatient*). Could someone open the windows, it's stifling in here.

ANDREW *scurries to the French windows and opens them wide*.

IKE (*to* STAGG). Are you aware of the consequences of postponing, even for as little as twenty-four hours?

STAGG. I think I am, sir.

IKE. Essentially I would be cancelling D-Day. Tuesday the 6th is logistically possible, but the period of daylight before low tide is over eighty minutes and would expose our troops to needless risk. The only other alternative this year, June 19th, is full of danger. No full moon, and more importantly we would need to dismbark three hundred thousand men who have been fully briefed. With the best will in the world, preserving the secret of D-Day would be impossible. Thousands of ships returning to harbour in stormy seas, corrosive uncertainty, demoralised men cooped up like animals on the way to the slaughterhouse.

STAGG *drops his head. It would seem that he has finally given up. The energy seeps out of him.*

Dr Stagg?

No response from STAGG.

Do you need some time out?

STAGG. No, sir. I understand.

STAGG *looks utterly defeated. But at this moment, the door opens and* KAY *enters, looking dusty and exhausted. She salutes the C-in-Cs.* IKE *glances at his watch.*

KAY. I'm sorry I'm late, sir.

IKE. Sit down, Lieutenant Summersby.

KAY *holds up an envelope.*

KAY. May I…?

IKE. Go ahead.

KAY *walks up to* STAGG *and hands him the envelope.*

STAGG. Excuse me.

STAGG *opens the envelope and takes out a piece of paper. He reads it, then folds it and returns it to the envelope.*

(*To* KAY.) Thank you.

IKE. Good news?

STAGG. No particular news.

IKE....okay.

IKE assesses STAGG for a moment, then continues.

Even if I support your view, Dr Stagg, I may still give the order to go. We've received information that the head of our code-breaking bureau in France has been captured by the Germans. We have no idea how much he has given away under Gestapo interrogation. If he cracks, years of planning and deception go up in smoke and Rommel will move his Panzer Divisions to Normandy. Any hold-up could be lethal. We cannot delay unless we absolutely have to.

Short silence. All eyes on STAGG.

STAGG. Sir...

Although superficially hesitant, there is strength in STAGG's next speech. His confidence starts to build.

Weather forecasting... is an imprecise science, but at best... it is... a science which combines the heart with the purity of physics. It has been a huge honour to be appointed Chief Meteorological Officer for the Allied Forces. It could be argued that this is the most important weather forecast in the history of warfare... and I am proud of that responsibility.

He turns to the chart.

I am now confident that the storm L6 will pass through the English Channel on Monday morning. It is a storm of unprecedented malignity for the time of year. I anticipate storm-force winds throughout the day.

IKE. You're certain?

STAGG. No, sir. I can't offer you certainty. I have always said that long-term forecasting is a gamble. What I offer is twenty-five years of observing British weather. Despite every risk you've identified, instinct and experience tell me that the landings should be postponed.

IKE. Okay... Okay...

IKE *walks to the French windows, his back to the room. Thinks for a moment, then turns.*

Assuming for a moment we trust Dr Stagg's prognosis – force-six winds, low cloud, considerable swell… what are the worst conditions we can tolerate? Bertie?

BERTIE RAMSAY. Anything above force five and the landing craft will capsize. Not just the troop carriers, but the LCTs and LCVPs carrying tanks and vehicles. Waves of four to six feet would be dangerous but tolerable. Anything over six feet inpossible. If Stagg's forecast is right, wind direction will be west-north-west causing wind against current. The subsequent swell must not exceed seven feet. My other concern is deterioration in the weather on Tuesday or Wednesday, which would leave a quarter of a million men stranded on the beaches with no possibility of landing more troops and equipment as back-up. (*To* STAGG.) Do you believe the weather could get worse on Tuesday and Wednesday?

STAGG. The weather could remain consistently as poor as Monday… unlikely though to be worse.

IKE. Trafford?

LEIGH-MALLORY (*to* STAGG). How complete would the cloud cover be on Monday morning?

STAGG. 10 10ths. Base: 0 to 500 feet.

LEIGH-MALLORY. Fog?

STAGG. Extremely likely.

LEIGH-MALLORY. Absolutely impossible. It would be a catastrophe. I won't be able to drop accurate markers for the gliders, so your flanks will be unprotected. My bombers won't be able to see their targets, so no guaranteed cover for the landings. Inaccurate bombing will put the lives of thousands of French civilians at risk. Under no circumstances could I support invasion in the conditions described by Dr Stagg.

IKE. Tooey?

SPAATZ. Everything Trafford says is true and if base is as low as zero, you're gonna get mid-air collisions – lose a lot of aircraft, a lot of lives. But if we get ashore, the war is over… may take a while, but it's over. Could argue that any sacrifice on Monday is justifiable.

Silence. IKE *walks round the room. All eyes are on him, but he is apparently oblivious to their presence as he struggles with his decision.*

IKE. Thank you, gentlemen. I am inclined… (*Long beat.*) to believe… to put my faith in… (*Another beat.*) Dr Stagg's forecast. And in that case I have no choice but to postpone Overlord by at least twenty-four hours. Compared with the enemy's forces, ours are not overwhelmingly strong.

We need every help our air superiority can give us. If the air cannot operate we must postpone. Are there any dissentient votes?

BERTIE RAMSAY. No.

LEIGH-MALLORY. No.

All eyes on SPAATZ.

IKE. Tooey?

They wait for SPAATZ*'s response.*

SPAATZ.…No.

IKE. So be it. D-Day will be postponed.

Blackout.

Scene Three

The following morning. 8.00 a.m. Sunday, 4 June 1944.

STAGG *wakes from fitful sleep. Everything very still. He hurries to the French windows and opens the shutters. Sunlight pours in. A beautiful morning.*

STAGG. Where are you? Where are you?

He opens the French windows and goes onto the balcony. The sound of a dog barking. Two men laughing. He scans the sky. North, east, south, west. He comes in from the balcony and taps the barometer. He checks the barograph, tearing off the circular strip of paper showing the readings. He examines them.

A breeze flicks the curtains. They billow slightly. STAGG notices. He watches eagerly for another gust, but the curtains settle again. Stillness.

Come on! Come on, come on!

The door opens. KAY *enters. She notices* STAGG's *uneaten supper on the table.*

KAY. You didn't eat.

STAGG. No.

KAY. Well, you missed something, it was rather good. Did you sleep?

STAGG *doesn't answer, he doesn't have to.*

No, neither did I.

Silence. STAGG *is staring out of the French windows, looking for any change, however small.*

Dr Forbes was extremely optimistic. The blood pressure is stable.

STAGG. It's no lower. The risk is the same.

KAY. But it hasn't gone up. He was optimistic, if it doesn't go any higher, and he sees no reason why it should, your wife will be fine.

STAGG *says nothing*.

Dr Stagg...

IKE *enters, smoking. He looks terrible – puffy-faced, bloodshot eyes, limping, etc*.

IKE. Where's your weather, Stagg? I took your advice, soldier, where's the fucking storm?

STAGG. A wee bit late, sir. It's coming.

IKE. It'd better be, you son of a bitch, or I'll string you up from the nearest lamp post.

STAGG *goes to the chart*. IKE *follows him*.

STAGG. Each red line marks the progress of storm L6. It's advancing as predicted. At four a.m. Ireland was experiencing severe gales. A little slower than I predicted. That's all.

IKE. But you're sure it's coming?

STAGG *takes a long time to answer.*

STAGG. Almost certain, sir.

They hold each other's gaze.

IKE. Almost.

The door opens. KRICK *enters. He salutes* IKE.

KRICK. Sir.

IKE. Irv. How are ya?

IKE *offers* KRICK *a Chesterfield*.

You smoking?

KRICK. I stopped, sir.

IKE. Good man. I'll smoke for you.

He lights a new cigarette with the tip of the old.

I still wanna get outside with that football.

KRICK. I'd like that, sir.

KRICK *goes to the French windows and opens the windows wide. He stands facing the balcony.*

You know, Ike, when I think of the United States of America, I see a quarterback. A fresh-faced, twenty-year-old quarterback.

IKE. I like that!

KRICK. He's an athlete, he has a sense of adventure, he's proud, he knows right from wrong, but he's not weighed down by his history or his past. When someone asks him to take a risk, he says, 'Why not?' He clears away the clutter and says, 'Yuh, I can do that.'

IKE. He may not be weighed down by his history, but you better believe he's weighed down by his responsibility. And by the time we've won this war, your twenty-year-old is gonna look old for his years.

IKE *slumps into a chair and closes his eyes.* KRICK *goes to one of his files and takes out the crucial 1923 analogue chart. He stands by the window, examining it.*

Long silence. Stillness.

Suddenly a strong gust of wind blows in from the balcony. The curtains billow and the analogue chart is blown out of KRICK*'s hands. He grabs at thin air, but the chart flies out of reach.*

The wind continues, strengthening with each gust. A cloud crosses the sun and the stage is instantly darker, colder.

STAGG *is profoundly relieved. He goes to the French windows and pushes the windows closed... as the first splash of gusty rain hits the glass.*

STAGG *turns to* IKE... *but he is fast asleep.*

Blackout.

Scene Four

Five hours later. 1300 GMT, June 4 1944.

The lights come up. Gusts of wind rattle the French windows on their hinges, rain hits the glass hard with each stormy gust. L6 has arrived.

The lights come up as the fourth chart unrolls. ANDREW *is at the top of the library steps.*

He climbs down, pushing the steps aside. The caption at the top of the new chart reads:

'1300 GMT, 4TH JUNE 1944.' Full of enthusiasm, ANDREW *pores over the new data, but* STAGG *sits hunched over his table, eyes closed, head throbbing, sapped of all energy.*

STAGG (*flatly*). What do you see?

ANDREW. 3, 4 and 5 have merged into Low 6.

STAGG. Aye.

ANDREW. High pressure over Greenland. 1023.

STAGG. Uh-huh.

ANDREW. Intense low off the north coast of Scotland.

STAGG. Aye.

ANDREW. L7 has intensified and enlarged east of
    Newfoundland – central pressure: 978.

    STAGG *says nothing. But his eyes flick open, animated for
    the first time in the scene.*

    High pressure, 1026, north of Hudson's Bay.

STAGG. Wait! Go back. What was the central pressure of L7?

ANDREW. 978.

STAGG. 978. Are you sure?

ANDREW. Absolutely.

    STAGG *is suddenly on his feet, standing beside* ANDREW
    in front of the new chart.

STAGG. L7 has hardly moved! 978. Look at the previous chart: 982! It's hardly moved at all... wait a minute... wait-a-minute! Andrew, I want the geostrophic in the warm sector.

ANDREW grabs a 'geostrophic scale' (a ruler), goes to the chart and takes measurements, while STAGG scribbles out an equation, murmuring the figures as he writes.

Po = p(1 − 0.0065 h over t x 0.0065 altitude plus 273.15) to the power of 5.257... All right... Po = 980(1-0.0065x10 over... 59.

ANDREW completes his measurement.

How fast?

ANDREW. 230 degrees. 50 knots.

STAGG. Storm force! L7 is slowing down, Andrew. There is just a chance...

A particularly strong gust of wind hits the French windows. The sound of something crashing down and breaking on the balcony.

ANDREW goes out to investigate. While he's out of the room, STAGG scribbles out another formula.

It *cannot* deepen much further.

When ANDREW returns, he's soaked. He's carrying a sheet of paper from the anemometer.

ANDREW. A tile came off the roof.

ANDREW lays the anemometer reading on a table. They pore over it.

They wouldn't have got anywhere near the beaches.

STAGG. Not tomorrow, no. But Tuesday morning... may be possible. Would Eisenhower go on Tuesday?

STAGG examines the chart.

(*Urgent.*) L7 is slowing. I need its speed. Get some of Ramsay's men up here. I want to know how many weather

ships we've got east of Newfoundland. I want radio
soundings from every base within five hundred miles of the
centre of L7. I need to know this storm's speed. Now.

He consults his watch.

Ten past one. We may be too late already. Andrew! Now.

ANDREW. Yes, sir.

ANDREW *races out. The* NAVAL METEOROLOGIST
hurries in with more readings. He puts papers on STAGG*'s
desk and leaves.* STAGG *scribbles another
incomprehensible equation on the chart.* KAY *enters.*

KAY. New chart, sir?

STAGG *is animated and focused.*

STAGG. There is just a chance, Miss Summersby... Just a
chance... the landings would have been impossible
tomorrow morning, that's certain. L6 won't clear the British
Isles till tomorrow evening at the earliest, the question is
how quickly the next storm, L7, will arrive? Look at this...

He points to L6's position.

L7 is dawdling, dragging its feet. Do you believe
Eisenhower would invade on Tuesday?

No chance for KAY *to answer, the phone rings.* STAGG
picks it up.

(*On phone.*) James Stagg...

A very long silence. STAGG *suddenly looks as if he's been
punched in the stomach. He reaches for a chair and literally
falls into it, poleaxed by the information he has received.*
KAY *watches him anxiously. The silence extends.*

...thank you... thank you for letting me know...

*He puts down the phone. His face is expressionless. A
moment of frozen time within the urgency of the scene.*

KAY (*nervous*). Who was that?

No response.

Dr Stagg? Was that the hospital?

But STAGG *summons all his resources and forces himself back on course, back to the subject of L7. Throughout the next conversation with* KAY, *he's writing down a stream of figures and calculations.*

STAGG. A storm of this malignity normally hurtles across the ocean. But it hasn't. Why not? The deceleration is dramatic. A fundamental shift in the upper-air structures overnight. We need as many radiosonde readings as possible, as soon as possible.

KAY. What are radiosondes?

STAGG. Balloon readings. High-altitude balloon readings. If upper-air currents have slowed overnight, there's a chance the gap between L6 and L7 will be long enough to provide a period of calmer weather on Tuesday, but if we get it wrong… if L7 arrives too soon, conditions could be even worse than today. We have to be as precise as it is possible to be.

The door opens and ANDREW *leads two Naval Meteorologists into the room.*

ANDREW. Commander Colin Franklin, Lieutenant David Battersby.

They salute STAGG.

FRANKLIN. How can we help?

STAGG *leads them to the chart.*

STAGG. L7 has slowed. I need to know how much. What have we got in the area?

FRANKLIN. Weather Obs has two launch sites on Newfoundland: 'C-har' and 'F-lab'. They're transmitting readings every 1000 feet up to 50,000. They're coming in at 0100, 0700, 1300 and 1800 hours.

STAGG *checks his watch.*

STAGG. The next readings are in five hours?

FRANKLIN. Yes, sir.

STAGG. Too late. Can you get me data outside synoptic hours? I need the information *now*.

FRANKLIN. I can try.

STAGG. Help yourself to a telephone.

FRANKLIN *sits and picks up a phone.*

(*To* BATTERSBY.) Weather ships?

BATTERSBY. Three of any use. Two American, one Canadian.

FRANKLIN (*on phone*). Could you give me radio soundings from 'C-har' or 'F-lab'? We need them now. Anything is valuable.

BATTERSBY *locates the weather ships' positions on the chart.*

BATTERSBY. *Dog*'s the closest. She must be near the eye of the storm. *Baker* is about six hundred miles north, and *How* is… here about five hundred miles south.

STAGG. Good. I want all their latest surface readings and any radio soundings they've got. Tell them we need them immediately.

BATTERSBY. Will do.

FRANKLIN *and* BATTERSBY *are now on the phone.* FRANKLIN *is already getting feedback.*

FRANKLIN (*hand over the receiver*). 'C-har's strongest upper wind was measured at 0830 hours – 310 degrees, 110 knots at 30,000.

STAGG. A drop of 30 knots in 8 hours. Andrew, get onto the weather ship east of Cork, get their latest speed for the jet stream.

FRANKLIN. 'F-lab' coming through… 0845 hours – 270 degrees, 85 knots at 25,000.

STAGG. Slowing.

BATTERSBY (*on phone*). Soundings for *Baker*, *Dog* and *How*, please.

FRANKLIN (*on phone*)....yes...

> FRANKLIN *is writing down figures.* ANDREW *picks up a phone.* BATTERSBY *waves a piece of paper in the air.* KAY *takes it and delivers it to* STAGG. STAGG *reads the figures.*

STAGG. Definitely slowing.

BATTERSBY (*on phone*). *Dog*: 250 degrees, 90 knots at 20,000...

ANDREW (*on phone*). 51.3 north, 12.5 west... 95 knots at 28,000...

BATTERSBY (*on phone*). *Baker*: 230 degrees, 85 knots at 25,000...

FRANKLIN (*on phone*). 90 knots, 15,000, 85 knots, 20,000...

BATTERSBY (*on phone*). 260 degrees, 102 knots at 18,000.

> BATTERSBY *holds up papers,* KAY *relays them to* STAGG. *It's at this moment that* KRICK *enters, into an atmosphere of urgent activity.*

> KRICK *watches for a moment from the door, then goes to* STAGG.

KRICK. What's up, buddy?

STAGG. L7 is decaying and filling...

KRICK. You think there'll be a gap?

STAGG. There could be.

> STAGG *hands* KRICK *a sheet of paper.*

Occlusion has started.

KRICK. The centre's drifting away from the triple point.

STAGG. Decaying rapidly. Central pressure – 978. What do you think?

KRICK. You could be right.

STAGG. Lieutenant Summersby, tell General Eisenhower I
need to speak to him. Urgently.

*STAGG turns back to the chart. ANDREW joins him. They
make further adjustments.*

*The storm outside is building constantly. The rain pounds
the windows.*

ANDREW. What do you think, sir?

STAGG. I think...

A surge of emotion overwhelms him, he struggles to control it.

I think...

But STAGG is too emotional to speak.

...we need more information. More information, Andrew.

*KAY returns with IKE. He's smoking. The storm outside
seems to weigh him down.*

IKE. You wanted to see me?

STAGG. A development, sir. Out of the ordinary.

IKE. Yuh?

STAGG. How long to turn the invasion force round again?

IKE. Have you seen the fucking weather?

STAGG. The storm east of Newfoundland is slowing down.
Enough to provide a window. A gap. A period of calmer
weather on the morning of Tuesday 6th.

*The wind screams outside and another roof tile crashes onto
the balcony as if to mock STAGG's instincts.*

IKE. Certain?

STAGG. Never certain.

IKE. Twenty-three landing craft capsized today returning to
port. Men drowned. One hundred and fifty thousand soldiers
trapped in their cabins. Seasick. Terrified.

STAGG. Aye… is Tuesday possible, sir?

IKE. Possible, but extremely risky.

STAGG. Information I'm receiving points to a gap between L6 and L7 long enough to launch the invasion on Tuesday morning.

IKE. Proof?

STAGG *consults his watch*.

STAGG. The next chart. Five hours.

IKE. Too late. I have to issue orders within an hour.

STAGG *is silent*.

Are you telling me to go?

STAGG. A calmer spell of weather will arrive tomorrow night. If you look at the chart…

IKE. I don't wanna look at the chart. I want you to look me in the eye. Tell me the weather's gonna be good on Tuesday morning.

A huge moment for STAGG.

STAGG. Good enough, sir.

IKE.…then I'm prepared to take the risk.

STAGG. I'm very confident. I've seen this happen before. Very confident.

IKE. You know there's a fucking hurricane blowing out there?

STAGG. It's not a hurricane, it's…

IKE *cuts him off*.

IKE. It's a helluva storm.

STAGG. Yes, sir.

IKE. Irving?

KRICK *looks up from his charts*.

KRICK. Tuesday morning… may be possible, sir.

IKE. Christ on the mountain, my weathermen agree! (*To* STAGG.) Good enough for the bombers?

STAGG. Yes, sir.

IKE. Cloud cover?

STAGG. Very little. 1 to 2 10ths.

IKE. Clear skies?

STAGG. Yes, sir.

IKE. Wind speed?

STAGG. Four occasionally five.

A beat, just the sound of the storm and the murmur of FRANKLIN, BATTERSBY *and* ANDREW *on the phone. Then:*

IKE. Okay. Goddammit! Okay, you son of a bitch, I'm gonna find the C-in-Cs and tell 'em your news.

IKE *goes to the door. He turns to the room.*

Good work, gentlemen. Thank you.

He leaves. ANDREW, FRANKLIN *and* BATTERSBY *continue to receive information on the phones.* KRICK *is surrounded by his charts.*

He searches for an analogous weather pattern from the past.

KAY *stands quietly by the chart.* STAGG *joins her.*

KAY. Was it news from the hospital?

STAGG. A son. I have a son. Born at 1100 hours. Sandy. Sandy Stagg.

Blackout.

Scene Five

Twelve hours later. 1 a.m. Monday, 5 June 1944.

The storm is louder and wilder.

STAGG *is alone, checking the chart for a final time.*

He goes to the French windows and forces the windows open. The storm rushes in, almost blowing him off his feet. He 'embraces' the wildness.

The door opens. KAY *enters. She's holding a plastic tray, carrying two plates of powdered scrambled egg, a jug of water and two glasses.*

KAY. As powdered eggs go, these are pretty good.

> *She puts the tray down on one of the tables and joins* STAGG *by the windows.*

> *The violence of the storm outside is extraordinary. The wind whips their hair and clothes.*

You believe you're right.

STAGG. I hope I'm right.

> STAGG *forces the French windows closed.* KAY *goes to the table and picks up the tray of food. She looks enquiringly at* STAGG.

> STAGG *clears space on the table and places a chair on each side. They sit opposite each other.* KAY *hands* STAGG *his scrambled egg. The storm is too loud for conversation.*

> *They eat.* KAY *pours water for them both. Coincidentally, they pick up their glasses at the same time. They catch each other's eye and clink glasses. They drink.*

> *More roof tiles crash onto the balcony outside. The rain batters the windows.* STAGG *goes to the French windows and closes the shutters. Pitch black for a second. He switches on a desk lamp. They continue to eat in silence.*

> *There's a knock on the door and* ANDREW *enters with the fifth chart.*

They all know how crucial it is. For a moment they don't move. Then STAGG *takes the chart. He and* ANDREW *wheel over the steps and hang it in silence.*

It rolls open. The final chart: '0100 GMT. JUNE 5 1944'. STAGG *takes one look at the chart … and has his answer.*

Slowly he climbs down the steps. His body feels profoundly heavy, his movements are jerky, as if his limbs won't obey orders. He lowers himself into a chair facing the audience. He stares out front. His face is rigid, impassive, giving away nothing.

KAY *doesn't know whether the news is good or bad. She looks at* ANDREW *imploringly.* ANDREW *walks over to* STAGG.

ANDREW (*extremely moved*). Congratulations, sir. Congratulations. Brilliant work.

STAGG *can't respond, unable to take in the scale of his achievement, like Alf Ramsay after winning the World Cup.* ANDREW *sees that* KAY *needs an explanation. He goes to the chart.*

(*To* KAY.) L7 has hardly moved. The storm has occluded above the triple point as Dr Stagg anticipated. L6 will leave the British shores shortly and a spell of calmer weather will move in tomorrow evening. The landings will be possible on Tuesday morning. The good weather will probably last twenty-four to thirty-six hours, after which stormy weather will return to the English Channel on Wednesday or Thursday.

The storm continues outside, as it has done all day. The lights close in on STAGG. *His expression: impassive, shocked. Close-up. Just his face…*

Blackout.

Scene Six

Twenty-two hours later. 11.45 p.m. Monday, 5 June 1944.

The wind has dropped – still blowing enough for the curtains to billow onstage, but it's a breeze, not a storm.

A camp bed has been set up. KAY and STAGG are onstage, and at last they are asleep. KAY is lying on the bed – stockinged feet, jacket wrapped round her as a blanket. STAGG is curled up on the floor, using his jacket as a pillow.

Then a sound: building and building in volume. Recognisable as fleets of bombers flying overhead, but now incomparably loud compared with the beginning of the play. An all-consuming sound.

KAY wakes. She sits up, bleary-eyed. Rested for the first time in weeks. She checks her watch and is amazed by what she reads.

KAY. No!

She swings off the bed and pads across the room, looking down at STAGG, still asleep. She goes to the French windows and opens them wide. She stares up at the bombers passing overhead. Wave after wave after wave.

Now STAGG is awake. He gets to his feet, joints stiff from lying on the floor. He joins KAY. They watch together.

STAGG. Very little cloud.

KAY. It's like the end of the world.

Silence.

It's nearly midnight.

STAGG is shocked. He checks his watch.

STAGG. Why didn't someone wake us?

KAY. Why should they? Nothing we can do now, Dr Stagg.

STAGG. Someone should have woken us though, surely?

Silence. They continue to watch.

KAY. The wind's dropped.

KAY pats STAGG on the back.

Aren't you clever?

Another silence.

I can't believe it. We've lived through Dunkirk. The Blitz. We've been cut off for so long and now finally it's happening... we're going to land on the Continent. Three years of listening to them all talking and planning and hoping and worrying... and now it's actually happening... I can't believe it. It's the beginning of the end.

The last of the bombers has passed overhead. The sound of their engines has faded to nothing. The door opens and IKE *enters. He looks as unslept as ever, but a weight has lifted off his shoulders.*

IKE. Well, it's on. No one can stop it now.

He holds up a paper bag.

I come bearing gifts.

He reaches into the bag and theatrically takes out:

Doughnuts! Three – jam – doughnuts.

He puts them on the table.

KAY. Where have you been?

IKE. Newbury, in Berkshire.

KAY. How did you get there?

IKE. I drove.

KAY. *You* drove?

IKE. Well, someone drove me.

KAY. Why didn't you wake me?

IKE. I couldn't wake you.

KAY. I drive you, Ike.

IKE. You looked so…

He tails off, censoring what he wants to say because of
STAGG.

You deserved to sleep.

KAY. Who drove you?

IKE. Brian somebody.

KAY. In my Packard?

IKE. No, in his Buick.

Short silence.

KAY. You should have woken me, Ike.

IKE. Help yourselves. Kay?

KAY *helps herself to a doughnut.*

Stagg, you gonna have a doughnut?

STAGG. I don't think I've ever had one.

IKE. Christ on the mountain, you haven't lived! Take one.

STAGG *takes a doughnut. He bites into it. Jam on his chin.*

What d'ya think, soldier?

STAGG (*mouth full*). Aye.

KAY. What were you doing in Newbury?

IKE. Visiting the 101st Airborne. My boys. I went to see them off.

STAGG*'s fingers and mouth are covered in jam and sugar.
He takes out a handkerchief and wipes his face.*

I ordered a car and Brian somebody drove me to Newbury.
Nobody knew I was coming. Nobody saw me drive there, no
stars on the plate, no flag on the hood, just an officer in a
motorcar. When we got there, General Maxwell wanted to
make a big thing of it, I said, 'No, let me just go out an' meet
the guys, talk to them, no big deal.' So that's what I did. Hard

to look a man in the eye when you know you may be sending him to his death. In every face I saw the schoolboy that soldier had once been. You know what I mean? When you see the child in the adult face. They were blackened up with boot polish and they looked like dirty, enthusiastic, serious-minded schoolboys on a summer camp. And they trusted me, their dads weren't there, so they were relying on me. There was one guy who leaned forward to catch every word I said, as if the words themselves would keep him safe. What could I say to them? What could I say to these... boys? I asked them how their chow was, asked them where they were from, I wanted to find a soldier from my home town, Abilene, these kids were from all over the United States, from Fort Worth, Little Rock, New York, Grand Island Nebraska, Blue Mound Kansas, Sunnyvale Texas, but no one from Abilene.

I don't know how they walk let alone run, they were loaded up like Christmas trees, anything they couldn't fit in their pockets they had strapped to their backs, their arms, their legs. There was one guy, he had a pack of Lucky Strikes taped to every available inch of flesh... but no Chesterfields. I gave him a pack... and we get the doughnuts!

IKE *pauses for a moment*.

The airborne divisions are... my baby. Trafford thinks I'm sending those boys to their deaths, but I believe their role will be pivotal... and that makes it personal. Those boys are *my* responsibility, they're risking their lives because I dug my heels in at a meeting in an office. That's really why I went to see them... and I will feel every one of their deaths.

Silence. The room is very quiet. IKE *checks his watch*.

They'll be landing in thirty minutes.

Another silence.

How did you like your doughnut?

STAGG. Aye.

IKE. What we need is something to wash them down.

STAGG. Ah… well…

STAGG pulls his suitcase into the middle of the room. He opens it.

Do you like whisky, sir?

IKE. Scotch whisky?

STAGG. Single-malt whisky.

IKE. You better believe it.

STAGG lifts out a full bottle of Talisker.

STAGG. Twelve-year-old Talisker. From the Island of Skye.

IKE. Goddamn! You gonna join us, Kay?

KAY. What do you think?

There's a pot of old coffee and cups on a table. KAY takes three of the cups and rinses them in the basin.

Will these do?

STAGG pulls out the cork stopper.

IKE. Mamie and I take summer vacations in Culzean Castle on the Ayreshire coast. Beautiful spot.

STAGG. When the war's over, sir, you must go to the Island of Skye.

IKE. We could drive up in the Packard, Kay.

KAY. I'd like that.

STAGG. Liz and I take a wee croft in the Red Hills. There's a granite pillar outside the front door called 'The Old Man of Storr', I've seen golden eagles perch on it… and a burn running through the garden, full of lumps of agate, the size of my fist. I love its weather, of course. Wind, rain, sunshine – all in a single day.

STAGG offers the neck of the bottle to IKE. IKE smells it.

IKE. Man! That'll clear your sinuses.

STAGG. Robert Louis Stevenson's favourite malt. 'The King o' drinks' he called it.

STAGG *pours whisky into the three cups.*

Water?

IKE. I'll have it neat.

STAGG. Lieutenant Summersby?

KAY. Half and half, please.

STAGG *does the honours and hands out the cups of Scotch.* IKE *holds up his cup.*

IKE (*murmured*). To every single man crossing the English Channel tonight. God be with them.

They hold up their white porcelain cups and drink.

My God! I can taste the peat.

STAGG. Aye.

IKE. Well, you've sold it to me, Stagg. Here's to the Island of Skye.

STAGG *tops up* IKE*'s glass.* IKE *checks his watch.*

Six hours.

He takes a slug of whisky.

Nobody knows where I am. I'm a king without a kingdom. Nothing I can do now. Over to Monty, Georgie Patton, Trafford, Bertie Ramsay…

Short silence.

But will they know we're coming? What if they've known all along? What if all the secrecy, the deception… fooled no one. Is Rommel in his bunker… licking his chops?

Instinctively, he looks at his watch again.

Six hours. Christ on the mountain.

KAY. I'd like to suggest a toast. To Dr Stagg's new baby.

IKE. Sure. Is it your first?

STAGG. No, two boys now.

IKE. We had two boys. John is twenty-two. He's just graduated from West Point.

STAGG. Following in his father's footsteps.

IKE. Yup. And we lost one… when he was four.

STAGG. I'm sorry.

IKE. Don't be. If someone asks me if I have kids, I always mention him. He's my eldest son. Always will be.

STAGG. My brother was killed in a motor accident when he was seventeen. I mention him too, of course most people would rather I didn't.

Short silence.

IKE. I miss him. Every day.

Another silence.

Tomorrow morning it could be two thousand, it could be ten thousand, it could be fifty thousand. Not 'if' but 'how many'. If we get ashore and lose ten thousand men it will be considered a price worth paying – it *will* be a price worth paying. I hope it's ten thousand not fifty. And here we are, mourning two deaths. Two losses. Each with its own chain reaction of grief. The brother, the sister, the wife… father, mother, friend… all scarred, all changed for ever. How many broken lives if fifty thousand die tomorrow? I couldn't command an army if I didn't believe in God.

He goes to the French windows and looks out into the darkness.

The wind's dropped.

He raises his cup to STAGG.

Thank you, Dr Stagg. What's your boy's name?

STAGG. Sandy.

IKE. To Sandy Stagg.

They raise their cups and drink. IKE *looks at his watch again.*

Jesus Christ. Five hours fifty-five minutes. Here's a curve ball, Stagg. You were going to tell me the rules of rugby union.

STAGG. Aye.

IKE. What the hell is happening on that pitch. You call it a pitch?

STAGG. Aye.

IKE. What's the objective?

STAGG *pours himself another Scotch.*

STAGG. To… carry the ball over the opposition's back line. The try line.

IKE. End zone. Yuh. What do you score for that?

STAGG. You score a try. Worth three points.

IKE. We score a touchdown. Six points… which is kind of ironic, because you don't have to touch the ball down to score a touchdown, you just have to cross into the end zone.

They take a sip of their whisky.

Can you kick the ball as well as throw it?

STAGG. Aye… but if you pass the ball with your hands you have to pass it backwards.

IKE *looks at* STAGG *steadily.*

IKE. Perverse.

STAGG. It's the most important rule.

IKE. Okay. Our quarterback, the commanding officer behind the linemen can throw it forwards, in fact he must throw it forwards. And a receiver will hopefully be in position to catch it. How many in a team?

STAGG. Fifteen. Eight forwards and seven backs.

IKE. We have seven linemen and four backs. And what is…

IKE *pours himself another Scotch and sits on the camp bed.*
He downs the Scotch in one, then decides to get comfortable
and lies on the bed on his back.

What is…

He links his fingers together to demonstrate.

…the 'formation' when the brutes huddle together and the
little guy throws the ball into the huddle.

STAGG. The scrummage.

IKE. We have a scrimmage.

STAGG. You have a scrimmage?

IKE. Sure. A scrimmage.

STAGG. We have a scrummage or scrum.

IKE. A scrum.

KAY. What are you two talking about?

IKE. When do you have a scrummage?

STAGG. Well… after a minor infringement of the rules… and
the 'little guy'… the scrum-half, feeds the ball into the
scrummage and redelivers it to the outsides.

IKE. Backwards?

STAGG. Backwards but running forwards.

KAY. It sounds like patting your head and rubbing your stomach.

IKE. Okay. That makes sense. See, I love watching any sport,
but in February, was it February? Yuh, February 1938,
Neville Chamberlain invited me to an England Scotland
match and I assumed I'd understand what the hell was going
on. American football, rugby union, same-shaped ball, same
origins – who was I kidding? It was like a foreign language.

STAGG *nods and sips his whisky.*

(*Closing his eyes. Silence, then.*) I wanted to coach. Well, I
wanted to play and then when my knee gave way, I wanted

to coach. I love football… I love it. There's nothing more beautiful to me than a quarterback looping a perfect forty-yard pass to a receiver in full flight. He arches into the air, defying gravity, catches the ball, floats 4 feet above the ground and lands softly in the end zone. Touchdown. Touch…

Silence. STAGG and KAY wait, but IKE is silent. Miraculously, he has fallen asleep. KAY puts her finger to her lips.

KAY. Sshhh.

She takes off her jacket and gently wraps it round IKE. STAGG watches. Something about the care she takes convinces him that she loves him.

Eventually KAY stands and turns away from IKE. She sees that STAGG is watching her. They hold each other's gaze.

What shall I do, Dr Stagg? What shall I do when the war is over and Ike goes back to Mamie? He says he's taking me with him. He wants me to become an American citizen and join the Women's Army Corps. He says we'll live in a clapboard house on Bear Mountain.

She shakes her head slowly, acknowledging the futility of the dream.

All this suffering, this terrible suffering… but I want the war to go on for ever.

KAY looks down at IKE. She rests her hand on his cheek for a second.

STAGG watches KAY watching IKE. He takes a sip of whisky.

KAY turns to STAGG. There is something complicit, something childlike when she whispers to STAGG:

Is there any more whisky?

STAGG. Aye. Bring me your cup.

KAY *quietly picks up her chair and places it alongside* STAGG's. *She sits and holds out her cup. He tops her up. She drinks.*

If tomorrow is successful, you'll go to France, won't you? With the family?

KAY. I'd like to see it through. I'd like to see Paris again. And Berlin, I've never been to Berlin, have you?

STAGG. No.

KAY. You'll go too. They'll need you. They'll want you to come, after all you've done. And now that Sandy Stagg is safely here, won't you want to go too?

STAGG. It's a huge honour. Aye, I'd like to see it through too.

STAGG *tops up his own cup. They glance at* IKE – *fast asleep.*

KAY. Why are you a weatherman? Does it run in the family?

STAGG. No. My father was the Duke of Buccleuch's personal plumber.

KAY. Really?

STAGG. He once took me into the Duke's garden, when I was a boy, it was pouring with rain. He pointed up at the guttering and said: you have to wait till it's really pouring to identify the leaks.

But all I could think about was: 'Why is it raining? Why are the clouds black? Why is the wind blowing?'

KAY. You know, weathermen are traditionally a bit boring.

STAGG. Are they?

KAY. Oh yes. But you're not, you're rather interesting.

STAGG. How could the weather ever be boring? It defines us. Rain, sun, wind... it feeds us, it keeps us alive, it can destroy us. To anticipate it, that's the challenge, that's the fascination. You can never second-guess nature, no matter how hard you try, no matter how much you know. And in two hundred years that will still be the case.

Short silence.

Liz tells me that the only time I talk is after a glass or two of Talisker.

KAY. It's terribly strong.

STAGG. Aye.

KAY. It stops burning after a while.

STAGG. It does.

KAY. Isn't it quiet? It hasn't been this quiet since we arrived. Everyone's holding their breath. Ike's probably the only one asleep in the whole building.

They look at IKE *for a moment, sleeping peacefully.*

What's the time?

STAGG (*checking his watch*). Quarter past twelve. D-Day.

KAY holds up her cup.

KAY. To us.

They clink cups, terribly quietly, so that the cups hardly touch.

STAGG. You'll have a child one day.

KAY is caught completely off-guard. She blushes. It takes her a moment to recover.

KAY (*challenging* STAGG). How do you know I want one?

STAGG says nothing, but looks at KAY *steadily.*

More whisky please.

STAGG. Water?

KAY. Noooo. There comes a point.

STAGG. Does there? Come a point?

KAY. There does. There comes a point when water in your whisky is completely irrelevant.

For the first time in the play, STAGG *laughs. The laugh is infectious,* KAY *laughs too. They giggle like children, trying not to wake* IKE. IKE *stirs and turns over.* KAY *puts her finger to her lips.*

Sssshhh.

STAGG. Ssshh.

For a moment, they look at each other in silence.

KAY. Everything you feel… is so… powerful in wartime. Every colour is so intense. Do you know what I mean?

Long silence. They drink whisky.

Stolen time… is always the best. When it's over, will you invite me to your house, to meet your two sons?

STAGG. Aye.

KAY. Good. I'd like that.

KAY *gets up and walks over to* IKE. *She's unsteady on her feet.*

(*Whispered back to* STAGG.) I'm… tipsy you know.

She looks down at IKE *sleeping.*

STAGG. I could sleep now.

KAY (*gentle*). Go to sleep, Dr Stagg.

And he does, he closes his eyes and drifts off. His cup of whisky is at an angle in his hand, close to spilling. KAY *returns and takes the glass out of his hand.*

She leans down and kisses his cheek.

She picks up her chair and places it beside IKE*'s bed. She sits, close to his head and watches over him.*

Blackout.

Scene Seven

The following morning. Tuesday, 6 June 1944.

When the lights come up, dawn is visible through the curtains.
IKE, STAGG *and* KAY *are all asleep.* KAY *has slid off her*
chair, onto her knees. Her head rests beside IKE*'s on the bed.*

Silence for a moment, then the door opens and CAPTAIN
JOHNS *enters. He takes in the scene and discreetly edges out of*
the room, clicking the door closed behind him. A beat, then
there is a loud knock on the door.

IKE *jolts awake, he leaps off the bed.* KAY *is up too.* IKE
groans as his knee, stiff from sleep, gives under him. KAY
straightens her hair. STAGG *stands up.* IKE *glances at his*
watch. All three are now alert.

IKE. Come in.

> CAPTAIN JOHNS *enters again. He slams to attention and*
> *salutes.*

CAPTAIN JOHNS. Good morning, sir!

IKE. Good morning.

> CAPTAIN JOHNS *unfolds a sheet of paper and holds it out*
> *to* IKE. IKE *stares at the paper, it's a long time before he*
> *takes it, but eventually he does. He puts on a pair of reading*
> *glasses. Silence as* IKE *reads. When he has finished, he*
> *lowers the sheet of paper and removes his glasses.*

IKE (*almost to himself*)....All major objectives achieved.

CAPTAIN JOHNS. May I be the first to congratulate you, sir.

IKE. A foothold established on all the beach heads?

CAPTAIN JOHNS. Yes, sir.

IKE (*hardly audible*). Thank you. Heavy casualties at Omaha?

CAPTAIN JOHNS. Yes, sir.

IKE. Do you have a figure?

CAPTAIN JOHNS. Not a precise figure, sir.

IKE. Approximately.

CAPTAIN JOHNS. In excess of four thousand.

IKE. At Omaha alone?

CAPTAIN JOHNS. Yes, sir.

IKE (*glancing through the paper again*). Nothing here about the airborne divisions.

CAPTAIN JOHNS. 82nd and 101st landed successfully. Pegasus Bridge has been secured.

IKE. Casualties?

CAPTAIN JOHNS. Minimal, sir.

IKE. Thank you.

> *A long silence, they all wait for* IKE*'s next move.* IKE *turns to* STAGG *and offers him his hand. They shake hands.*

Thank you so much, Dr Stagg. You've stretched yourself to the limit, soldier. I want you to go back to your family, get to know your son, sort out those bags under your eyes. Couldn't have done it without you. I wanna thank you from the bottom of my heart.

STAGG. You won't be… requiring me to…

IKE. No. You need to stop. Enough is enough. I'm not taking you to France.

> IKE *allows* STAGG *a second to respond, but* STAGG *can't find any words.*

I think Irving Krick has a lot of catching up to do, don't you? He owes me. I wanna use a bit of his Yankee bounce in the months ahead. Nothing personal, you need a rest and Irv needs a kick up the ass. I'm gonna take him with me to Berlin, make sure he gets it right next time. You did a great job.

> *In essence,* STAGG *has been sacked.* IKE *turns to* KAY.

(*Very formal, distant.*) You both did. Very, grateful,
Lieutenant Summersby. Would you excuse me?

For KAY, IKE's *formality is a chill wind. With no further
ado,* IKE *leaves.* CAPTAIN JOHNS *follows him out. The
door closes.* STAGG *and* KAY *are alone.*

KAY (*murmured*)....Would you excuse me...

A long silence. Both of them shocked. Eventually KAY *turns
to* STAGG.

I want you to remember this. You are *twice* the man Colonel
Krick will ever be. He's a salesman, he's all 'surface'. I
know nothing about the weather, but I know that. You saved
the day. Remember that, please.

STAGG *says nothing. Another silence, then* STAGG *notices
a piece of paper lying on the bed. A piece of paper which has
fallen out of* IKE's *pocket.* STAGG *picks it up and reads it.*

STAGG. Well. He won't need this.

STAGG *reads it to* KAY.

(*Reading.*) 'Our landings in Normandy have failed to gain a
satisfactory foothold and I have withdrawn the troops.

My decision to attack at this time and place was based upon
the best information available. The troops, the air and the
Navy did all that bravery and devotion to duty could do. If
any blame or fault attaches to the attempt it is mine alone.'

KAY *is very moved.*

KAY. That's my handwriting you know.

STAGG *looks up from the paper.*

Ike dictated it to me yesterday. He had a terrible headache, his
knee was hurting... he was convinced the invasion would fail.

STAGG *turns the paper over.*

STAGG. There's a drawing on the back.

KAY. Oh, that's our clapboard house on Bear Mountain. Artist's impression.

STAGG. Did you do it?

KAY nods.

(*Genuine.*) Very good.

KAY. It seemed to cheer him up.

STAGG holds out the sheet of paper to KAY.

STAGG. Why don't you keep it?

KAY. Do you think I could?

STAGG. Put it in your pocket. Go on.

KAY. I think I will.

She takes the paper, folds it and slips it into her pocket. They smile.

You must get home, Dr Stagg.

STAGG. Aye.

KAY. Will you send my regards to your wife, and to Sandy, of course.

STAGG. I will.

KAY. I like you very much. You're a good man.

Silence. STAGG offers KAY his hand. They shake hands.

STAGG. Good luck, Miss Summersby.

KAY. Thank you.

Silence.

I'd better go and see if I can help.

KAY goes to the door, then turns to STAGG.

It's all… wonderful news.

Her heart breaks. She leaves, closing the door. STAGG
stands, motionless for a second, then walks over to the chart.

He looks for a last time at the network of isobars and curves,
fronts and occlusions. Then carefully, gently, he touches the
chart, placing his hand over the storm L6.

The lights fade.

The End.

www.nickhernbooks.co.uk

facebook.com/nickhernbooks

twitter.com/nickhernbooks